Praise for

YESSS!

"This is a truly brilliant book, written by a truly great guy! You won't want to miss the amazing advice and life hacks that this book gives to you. All written in an easy to access, fun to read way it will help you win at life. My own boys have read it and they've all given it a five star review! This book helps you to live life to the fullest and enjoy the journey along the way. Thanks for the ideas and help for our children, Paul. Having worked with young people for over 25 years in both sport and education, this is quite simply a MUST read!"

DREW POVEY,
from Channel 4's series *Educating Greater Manchester*

"Paul's wonderful book, crammed with insight, actions, humour and hope will help you to create a better future, not only for yourself but for all of us."

RICHARD GERVER,
Speaker, author and education expert

"A hugely helpful book for both young people and adults alike. I loved it."

DR KATE MIDDLETON,
Psychologist and director of the Mind & Soul Foundation

YESSS!

The S.U.M.O. Secrets
to being a
Positive, Confident Teenager

Paul McGee

Illustrated by Fiona Osborne

WILEY

Library of Congress Cataloging-in-Publication Data

A catalogue record for this book is available from the British Library.

ISBN 9780857088710 (paperback)
ISBN 9780857088758 (ebk)
ISBN 9780857088741 (ebk)

10 9 8 7 6 5 4 3

Cover and Illustrations by Fiona Osborne

Set in 12/16 pt BioRhyme by SPi Global, Chennai, India
Printed in Great Britain by Bell and Bain Ltd, Glasgow

Ever had a book dedicated to you before?

Well you have now.

This book is dedicated to you.

And your future.

CONTENTS

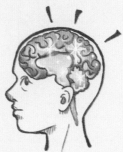

ix

A Quick HELLO From Me

Hello. The chances are we have never met, but
I wanted to say hi and let you know why I've written
this book and also a little bit about me.

But first, a question.

What gets you excited?

Is it Christmas or your
birthday? What about
going on holiday?
Maybe it's going to see
your favourite singer
or performer?

Lot's of things excite me. Going to football matches can give me a real buzz – particularly if it's a stadium I haven't been to before and there's a big crowd. I also get excited about travelling to new places – especially if I know there'll be sunshine when I arrive!

But do you know what has consumed me with excitement these last few weeks?

Writing this book.

Seriously, the more I've researched the topic and spoken to other people, the more excited I've become. I just wish I'd known some of these ideas when I was a teenager, because it took me years to discover these 'secrets' and they've had a massive impact on my life and I know on other people's lives too.

And trust me, they will have a great impact on you too. Not because you have simply read the book, but because of what you'll do with the stuff you'll learn. That gets me really excited.

So, what do you think of the title of the book? It's pretty short and simple isn't it (a bit like me really). 👀

Here's why the book is called

I believe reading this book will help you to say:

 to ... Embracing adventure and life's possibilities.

 to ... Being more curious.

 to ... Exploring this amazing planet.

 to . . . Making the most of your potential.

 to . . . Asking for help.

 to . . . Believing in yourself.

 to . . . Making a difference to the planet.

 to . . . Questioning and sometimes challenging adults.

 to . . . Aiming high.

 **YESSS!** to . . . Not giving up.

 **YESSS!** to . . . Exploring other people's perspectives.

 **YESSS!** to . . . Helping and encouraging others.

 **YESSS!** to . . . Learning – even when you've left school.

 **YESSS!** to . . . Being kind to yourself AND others.

 **YESSS!** to . . . LIFE!

My guess is the person who gave you this book

wants you to say **YESSS!** to those things too.

Hopefully, by the time you've finished the book, you'll be thanking them because they gave it to you.

The subtitle includes the words 'The SUMO Secrets'. I don't know about you, but when someone says 'Can I tell you a secret?' my reply is never 'No thanks I'd prefer not to know'.

The word 'secret' instantly gets my interest. I'm curious to discover some information that others don't know.

This book contains six big secrets that, it's fair to say, I didn't know when I was a teenager. I really wish I had, though, and as you read the book, I'm sure you'll understand why. You'll be discovering ideas and learning things that a lot of people, including adults, are not always aware of. I've also included a few little secrets throughout the book, too, and my aim is that as many people as possible discover these secrets. That's why I'm excited to hear from you about what you've learnt and, more importantly, what you've done as a result of reading this book.

Being a teen can be a really exciting and enjoyable time. You're moving away from being a child and growing into an adult. But it can also be a tricky and sometimes really challenging time too. Leaving primary school and going to secondary school can be a big jump, as you'll have discovered if you've done that already.

And there's soooooo much changing about you physically, both on the inside and the outside, as you experience the effects of both puberty and adolescence. In a nutshell: you're becoming an adult.

During this time, we are also developing our identity, building new friendships and realising that at times we prefer being with our friends more than we do our parents or other adults.

The bottom line?

A lot is changing.

Which is normal.

But it can also be a bit difficult at times too. (To be fair, being an adult can be a bit of a challenge as well.)

So you were probably given this book to help you understand yourself a little more and to give you some tips and tools on how to not only survive these interesting times in your life, but also to thrive through them too.

Oh, and by the way, although this book is aimed at teenagers, lots of adults could probably benefit from reading it too. So, if you read something you think they need to know, make sure you point it out to them.

Before we get started on our journey together, here's a few things about me.

17 THINGS ABOUT THE BLOKE WRITING THIS BOOK

1. When I was born there were no McDonald's in the UK. Seriously. Zero. Zilch. The first McDonald's wasn't opened until I was 10 years old. (So if you want to know what year I was born, you'll have to find out the year McDonald's first opened in the UK.)

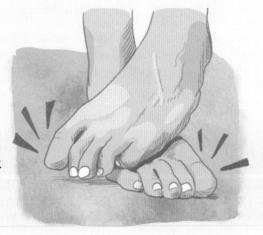

2. I've had both my big toenails surgically removed. (I hope you aren't eating any food at the moment ⊙⊙.)

3. When I was growing up, if we went on holiday (which wasn't often, although I did go to the Isle of Wight once), we had to carry our suitcases. They didn't have wheels on them, or a pull-up handle.

S.U.M.O. Challenge

Ask an adult if they remember when suitcases had no wheels. And check out the length of their arms too. If they've got really long arms, they probably spent a lot of time carrying suitcases when they were younger.

4. My Mum and Dad divorced when I was 5. The stepfather I ended up with was not a great bloke. I had some happy times as a teenager, but a lot of my unhappy times were due to him 🙁.

5. I loved English and Drama at school, but struggled with Maths and Science – particularly Physics. I once got 7% – yep, you read that right, 7% on a Physics exam.

6. When I left school, I worked in a bank in Manchester. A qualification in Physics was not required. Unfortunately, I hated the job. I was like a lizard on an iceberg. It wasn't a place I enjoyed or an environment where I could thrive.

7. I ended up going to Bradford University where I studied Psychology and developed a love of curry.

8. During a summer break from university, I did street theatre in Hollywood, Los Angeles. Unfortunately, I wasn't spotted by a talent scout, so went home to continue my degree and eat curry.

9. After leaving university, I started working in a beefburger factory but became ill and lost my job. I don't think the beefburgers caused it.

My illness was called ME or Chronic Fatigue Syndrome and it meant I had no energy and always felt exhausted. It was like charging your phone all night and waking up to find it had only 5% charge. I slept a lot and felt like I was missing out on life.

10. I eventually began to feel a little better and tried to get a job, but no one would hire me as I couldn't pass a medical. So, I hired myself. I was amazing at the interview ⌣.

11. I now speak at conferences in the UK and abroad in places like Australia, America, Asia and Africa – as well as a few places that don't begin with 'A'.

12. I work with a Premier League football team. Want to know which team it is? Your clue is that they won the Premier League by scoring a goal in the last minute of their final game of the season. The guy who scored it was from Argentina. OK, that's enough clues. If you still don't know the answer, contact me via email at yesss@thesumoguy.com or via Instagram @theSumoguy and I'll tell you.

13. I've written 11 books so far which have all been for adults. This is my first one aimed at younger people like you. I guess what you think of this one might mean it's my last – but hopefully not.

14. I love animals and have two cats, Louis and Milo. I enjoy talking to them first thing in the morning, although they tend to look at me with an expression that says 'Cut the chat mate, we're not interested. Give us the food and throw in a few treats whilst you're at it.'

(If there was a cat division of the SAS, Milo, my younger cat, would be a member. Louis, however, reminds me of me when I was younger – he loves his food and likes to sleep all day.)

15. I once did a bungee jump in New Zealand and wasn't scared. What does scare me though is slipping on ice! I'm paranoid about slipping in icy weather, or when there are loads of damp leaves on the pavement.

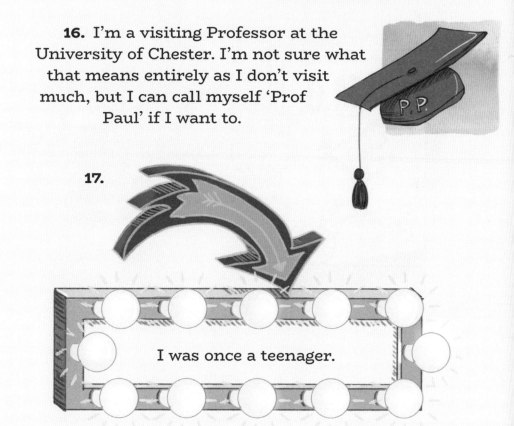

I'm not saying I've got a poor sense of balance, but seeing me walk in icy conditions is the equivalent of watching a giraffe coming down a mountain on roller skates.

16. I'm a visiting Professor at the University of Chester. I'm not sure what that means entirely as I don't visit much, but I can call myself 'Prof Paul' if I want to.

P.P.

17.

I was once a teenager.

In 2005 I wrote a book called *SUMO (Shut Up, Move On)* – *the straight talking guide to creating and enjoying a brilliant life.* We'll be exploring some of the ideas from that book in this one. The words 'Shut Up' were not meant to be aggressive, but some people thought they were, so SUMO can also stand for Stop, Understand, Move On. Lots of people forget my name, so they just call me 'The SUMO Guy' or just 'SUMO'. My mum still calls me Paul though as she's got a good memory.

There's Something AMAZING Inside You!

●●●

OK, it's quiz time. Ever thought about what is the most complex thing in the world?

The Large Hadron Collider? Nope.

The inside of the world's largest telescope? Nope.

Any thoughts?

Well, guess what? The most complex thing in the whole world is inside your head.

It's your brain.

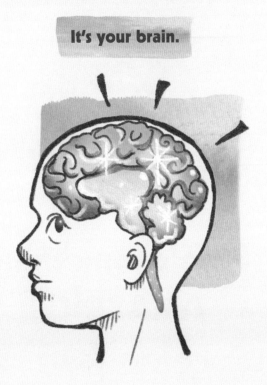

Trust me, it's amazing and we're learning more about it now due to all the fantastic things scientists are developing in order to study it.

Now, in order to understand ourselves and other people, it's really helpful to learn more about how our brains work. The brain is incredibly complex, so in order to simplify our understanding we often use a model.

A very smart guy called Daniel Kahneman wrote a book called *Thinking, Fast and Slow* which has sold over 2 million copies. Impressive eh?

In the book he talks about two systems or departments in your brain. Your fast system and your slow system.

He makes understanding your brain really simple and I'd like to develop our friend Daniel's idea (using baseball caps!) in order to understand why all people behave the way they do . . . including you.

So, imagine your brain being divided into two sections. One is the fast part of your brain, the other the slow part. Now imagine each section wearing a coloured baseball cap. One part wears a red baseball cap and the other a blue one. Any idea what colour your fast brain is wearing?

If you said 'Red',
you're right.
Congratulations!

If you said 'Blue', have
another guess . . .

Now this may sound a little too simple, talking about different coloured baseball caps to describe parts of your brain, but I do this with adults including teachers and they find it helpful. In fact, I do work with doctors who know a lot about this stuff and when I'm speaking about Red and Blue Caps, they don't start shouting

'You're a fraud, you haven't got a clue what you're talking about Paul'.

Well not to my face anyway.

So, let's find out a little more about your Red and Blue Cap Brains.

This is the oldest part of your brain. When you were growing, in your mum's womb, this was the bit of the brain that developed first. It's sometimes called our primitive and emotional brain.

One of its main priorities is to keep us alive and also pursue things that bring us pleasure. Guess how long we humans (or Homo sapiens) have been strutting our stuff on planet Earth?

Any ideas? 20,000 years? 50,000? 100,000?

Maybe ask an adult if they know. I bet loads won't.

It's actually between 150,000 to 200,000 years. Now if the adults didn't get the right answer, please don't laugh at them and call them a loser – OK? They might be grown up, but that doesn't mean they know everything – despite what they tell you! ☺

Now, if they did get it right, that's pretty impressive. They deserve a high five or a fist bump, or if that's too much, at least a little smile.

Please don't say . . .

'What a loser. Fancy knowing the answer to that question. You need to get out more.'

Seriously, don't say that! ☺

HERE'S SOME THINGS ABOUT YOUR RED CAP (FAST) BRAIN.

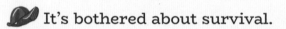 It reacts fast to situations. It makes a choice even when it has not got all the facts.

Why?

Because one of its main purposes is to keep you alive.

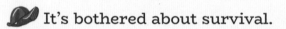 It's not bothered initially about free Wi-Fi.

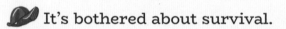 It's bothered about survival.

Over 150,000 years ago, your ancestors and mine weren't so concerned about how many Instagram followers they had or how to take the perfect selfie. They were more concerned about not getting eaten by an animal such as a tiger, woolly mammoth or an elite member of the SAS cat division.

Your Red Cap Brain developed what we call a fight or flight response.

What does that mean?

When faced by a threat from a predator who is looking for food in order to survive – and you could be the main dish on the menu – either get a group of your mates together and fight for your lives, or get your running shoes on and flee for your life.

Remember: you don't have to run faster than the deadly predator – just run faster than one of your mates!

That's how you stayed alive over 150,000 years ago.

So, your Red Cap Brain acts without thinking. It's impulsive. It goes with its initial feeling, even when it doesn't have all the information. It guesses a lot of the time.

And that was useful sometimes.

Why?

Well imagine you and your mate Colin (Colin was a very popular name 150,000 years ago, honest) were having an afternoon walk after eating a woolly mammoth burger and fries earlier.

Suddenly you hear a rustle in one of the bushes nearby.

What do you do?

You react. It could be a saber-toothed tiger. You could be its dinner. No more woolly mammoth burgers for you. Your life would be over before you knew it.

You and Colin have no time to waste.

You must act.

Fight or flight?

Either way, you don't stand there contemplating if this would make a great photo opportunity, whether you should FaceTime a friend or let your WhatsApp group know the predicament you're in. There's no time.

That's why Red Cap (Fast) Brain is crucial. Now of course you and Colin might run away and then realise there was no saber-toothed tiger. It was just the wind (and to be fair, Colin does have a wind problem, which probably explains a lot about why you're his only friend).

So you reacted without having all the facts and were wrong.

Hey ho.

But at least you're still alive.

You don't want to be like your mate Sunita, the most laid-back 'no worries' friend you know.

Sunita's problem was that when she heard a sound in the bushes, she thought 'that's just Colin dealing with the effects of his burger'.

Maybe it was.

But what if Sunita was wrong?

What if it was a saber-toothed tiger?

That might explain why you haven't seen a lot of Sunita recently.

So, do you see how Red Cap Brain would rather be safe than sorry? Sometimes it will be wrong – but at least it's safe.

Now all this happened over 150,000 years ago, before your Gran and Grandad were even born – and I know they're ancient. But here's the thing.

We all still have a Red Cap Fast Brain now, all these years later.

Yep, inside every person on this planet is an inner cave dweller.

SO WHAT ABOUT OUR **BLUE** CAP?

Your slow brain, Blue Cap, is your thinking brain. We use it to plan, reflect and analyse in order to make decisions.

When Red Cap needs help, it calls upon Blue Cap – some of the time.

So, imagine if you're given the following question:

The likelihood is your immediate answer is 4.
You automatically knew. You didn't have to think
about it. That's **Red** Cap working.

But what if you got this question:

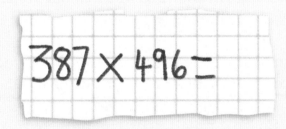

Now you have to stop and think. (If you didn't, then
you're a mathematical genius!)

You're now engaging the Blue Cap thinking part of your brain, but when you do so this takes more time and more effort than when you're using your Red Cap.

And here's the thing about your brain – it uses a lot of energy. So, if it can save energy it will – and when Red Cap is running the show, it's more likely to take the comfortable, easy, energy efficient, fast route.

The problem is, when it does so, it doesn't always make the best choices and can get things wrong.

Here's a great example of that.

Here's what seems a simple challenge that our friend Daniel Kahneman talks about in his book *Thinking, Fast and Slow.*

A bat and a ball together cost £1.10. Now the bat costs exactly £1 more than the ball.

So how much does the ball cost?

What do you reckon?

Most people, including adults, say the ball costs 10 pence.

But that's not right.

The ball costs 5 pence.

Don't believe me?

Let's do the maths.

If we assume the ball costs 5 pence and the bat costs £1 more, the bat would cost £1.05.

£1.05 + 5p = £1.10. Ta da!

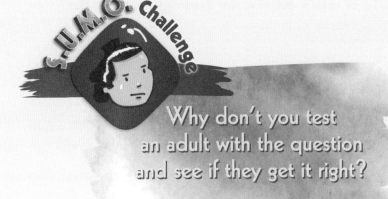

Why don't you test an adult with the question and see if they get it right?

So, your **Red** Cap Brain jumps to conclusions, goes with its initial reaction and speed counts more than accuracy.

These are traits that helped us survive on the African Savannah over 150,000 years ago. And sometimes your Red Cap Brain reactions are right. But sometimes they're not and they don't always help us in today's modern world, particularly when technology means we can respond so quickly to messages we get from our mates.

Instant messaging can lead to instant escalation

Trust me, engaging Blue Cap and allowing ourselves time to slow down and process what others say or do could save us so much hassle.

HERE ARE THREE THINGS TO BE AWARE OF WHEN RED CAP IS IN CONTROL:

1. We worry about things that don't actually happen.

2. We believe 'if I think it, it must be true'.

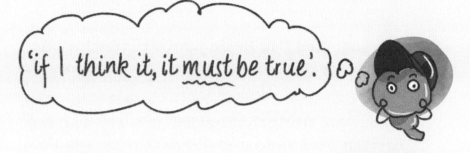

'if I think it, it must be true'.

3. We believe 'if I feel anxious, there must be danger'.

little S.U.M.O. Thought

Don't believe everything you think

The media have one goal – to get our attention. And the easiest way to do that? Make us fearful or make us angry. And how do they do that? By appealing to our **Red** Cap Fast Brain. Trust me, it's understandable why young people and adults can get stressed by reading the news headlines sometimes.

In a nutshell, our **Red** Cap Brain is always keeping careful watch for possible danger or difficulties, but can at times cause us to be worried and anxious about imaginary things.

As a result, we can feel anxious about trying or experiencing new things. It's OK to have uncertain feelings, but if we're to say YESSS to new opportunities, we need to make sure our **Blue** Cap Brain helps us calm down and get a sense of perspective. Whether that new thing is going to new places, taking up a new hobby, travelling on your own somewhere or deciding to make friends with someone you don't know, that's all part of saying YESSS to life!

And our **Blue** Cap Brain wants to have its say, but remember:

We access Blue Cap Brain when we decide to slow down and intentionally use it

And how are you going to do that? Stay tuned because that's what the rest of the book is about.

Finally, here's another way to think of our **Red** and **Blue** Cap Brains. Imagine in a car, **Red** Cap is the accelerator and **Blue** Cap is the brake. You need both in order to drive safely – and if we are going to enjoy our journey on this planet and travel well, we need both parts of our brain working well together.

So let's do a summary of each of our **Red** and **Blue** Cap Brains and what they are responsible for.

RED CAP FAST BRAIN	BLUE CAP SLOW BRAIN
Threat detector – sometimes sees threats that aren't there. Still, better to be safe than sorry	Thinks long term
Driven by feelings and emotions and the pursuit of pleasure	Rational and logical
Reactive and impulsive	Weighs up options – 'Let's explore this more'
Values speed over accuracy	Analyses
Jumps to conclusions without having all the facts	Reflects
Bothered about satisfying its feelings now in the moment	Plans
Not bothered about or even considered what might happen in the future	Considers other people's perspective
	Aims to stop us doing stupid things

One final thing to be aware of before we explore the rest of our SUMO Secrets is this. When we're going through our teenage years, a lot is happening in our brains. Blue Cap Brain is not fully developed yet so it still has a lot of work to do to influence Red Cap. (In fact, it is not fully developed in most people till our mid 20s!) Sometimes it's like Red Cap is dominating completely – and it will, unless you learn how to manage it . . . and that's where our next five SUMO Secrets will really help.

BLUE CAP BRAIN REFLECTION TIME

🎣 Can you think of a time when you were concerned or anxious about something but it ended up being OK?

🎣 Have you ever made a decision about someone but then later changed your opinion of them? (If so, maybe that's because Red Cap Brain jumped to conclusions too quickly.)

🎣 Which of your mates can you run faster than? 😊

The MAGIC Formula

OK, so you may remember from my introduction that Physics and Maths weren't my strong subjects at school. (Although I did even worse in my Pottery exam, when my pot blew up in the kiln and I didn't even get a mark.) However, this does go to show that doing badly in an exam doesn't have to ruin the rest of your life.

So, mentioning the word 'formula' to me is not something that puts me at ease. It evokes dark memories from my distant past, of Maths and Physics lessons. However, a few years ago, I heard someone explain a formula that has literally changed my life.

Here's how I came across it.

Sitting comfortably?

Good, I'll begin.

It was a summer day in Manchester. In other words:

it was raining,

but at least the rain was warm. I was in my bright red 1.1L Ford Fiesta – which I guess is the equivalent of driving a Ferrari today. I think. (Cars aren't my strong point.) I was taking my wife Helen to Wigan for a romantic lunch of pie, chips and a deep-fried Mars bar. We were listening to a cassette tape as we drove and discussing whether to add curry sauce or mushy peas to our food order.

Now I realise you've never heard of cassette tapes, which is hardly surprising as they became extinct shortly after the dinosaurs died out. However, they were like a CD. If you're still not sure what I'm on about, please ask someone to explain – preferably the oldest person you know. (Your Geography teacher perhaps?) And if you would prefer not to ask anyone but you're still curious to know what they were, go on to YouTube and search for 'what are cassette tapes?'

Anyway – there was a guy called Jack Canfield talking on the cassette tape about how to get the most out of life. To be honest, what he was saying wasn't that interesting and Helen had fallen asleep, which was confirmed by the noises she was making. I'm not saying they were strange, but at one stage I thought there was a problem with our car engine.

However, while Helen was dreaming of deep-fried Mars bars, Jack suddenly said something that got my attention.

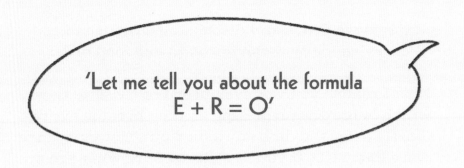

'Let me tell you about the formula
E + R = O'

Now the only formula I had come across at the time was from a German bloke called Albert Einstein – who as you'll know was a very clever guy (although his hair needed more gel on it in my opinion).

hey!

He had talked about $E = MC^2$ which had something to do with space and time. Jack's formula was a little easier to understand though (well to me, anyway). It was simply this

E + R = O

He then went on to explain what each letter stood for.

Event + Response = Outcome

Now you're probably thinking –
what, and this formula changed your life?
Seriously?

Yep!

Let me explain . . .

Jack talked about how 'Events' happen to us in life. For instance, you might have something horrible said about you or let's say at school you receive a piece of homework back from the teacher with the worst mark in the class and your mates laugh at you.

Jack's point is that the outcome doesn't automatically happen because of the event — it happens because of our response to it.

Let's test Jack's theory and see if some events in your life could have had a different outcome if you'd responded differently.

THE

Somebody says something horrible about you online. 🙁

 Possible Responses	Possible Outcomes
◘ Believe what they said is probably true and spend time alone dwelling on it	
◘ Get upset and decide to talk to a friend	
◘ Get upset and decide to say something horrible back	
◘ Get upset and talk to an older person about what happened (older sibling, a friend from a higher year)	

- Contact the person and ask them why they said what they said

- Decide this person's opinion is not important and choose to ignore it

It's interesting isn't it? The same event could lead to a different outcome. Yet I wonder if you can relate to the following:

For many years I would think that the outcomes to whatever happened to me in life were nothing to do with me – they just happened. So I thought

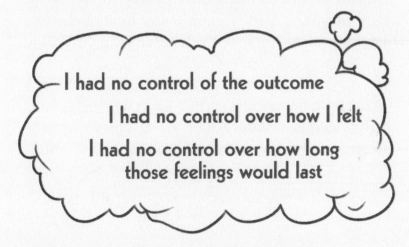

I had no control of the outcome

I had no control over how I felt

I had no control over how long those feelings would last

So, if life went well, then great. If people were kind, that would make me happy. But what if life didn't go well? What if people weren't kind?

My response was to play my BSE card.

Now it isn't great when life doesn't go well. In fact, life can be tough and some pretty lousy things can happen. And if people say or do horrible things, that isn't good. I'm not saying you should pretend it is.

And let's be honest, what I am saying is not always easy to do. After all, if you're upset over something – which colour cap is your brain wearing?

It's your Red Cap.

But when we're emotional, when we're angry or sad, remember our Red Cap Brain isn't good at thinking clearly. It reacts.

And it jumps to conclusions. One of the conclusions it can jump to sometimes is:

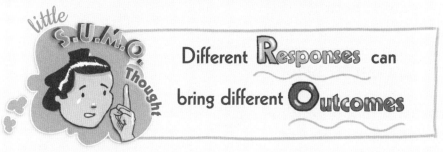

I have no choice. How I'm feeling is everyone else's fault.

That's how I used to think and act. In fact, I was well into my 30s before I listened to Jack and learnt about his formula.

Now I'm not saying it is easy to respond well. Tapping into your Blue Cap thinking can be hard. And it can be very hard when you're upset. That's why ALL the SUMO Secrets will be important for you to discover in order to help yourself.

But to start with, just try and remember, the formula is not $E = O$.

If it was, that would mean that everyone has the same outcome to an event as you do. When actually they don't.

little S.U.M.O. Thought

Different Responses can bring different Outcomes

Let's look at another 'Event' and how different responses could lead to different outcomes.

THE Event

You receive the worst mark in your class and your mates laugh at you.

Possible Responses	Possible Outcomes
Be upset and tell yourself you're stupid and not very good at this subject	
Blame the teacher	
Pretend you're not bothered and laugh about it	
Talk to the teacher and ask for help	
Talk to a friend or someone older to see if they can help	

This is really important to remember. . .

So much of what happens in life is influenced by our **Responses**.

Sometimes we might not succeed at something straight away or we receive a bad mark and get laughed at by friends. When this happens, we have a choice. We could decide to give up or decide to get help and keep trying.

As my great friend Drew Povey says. . .

Whatever the day of the week, every day is a 'Chooseday'

Here's an example of someone who kept on trying.

Whether you play sport or not, I think you'll find this story interesting.

You may have heard of the footballer David Beckham. (His wife Victoria used to be a singer and is now a successful businesswoman.) He played for

lots of teams including Manchester United,
Real Madrid and Preston North End
(seriously, that's no joke).

He also played for his country, England, and in
2001 (which I realise is a long time ago), they played
Greece in a World Cup qualifier at Old Trafford.
(Wembley Stadium was being rebuilt at the time.)

England were favourites to win but Greece played
really well.

My son Matt and I were at the game. The
atmosphere had been great to begin with, but with
one minute of the match to go, England were losing
2–1. If the score stayed the same, they were not
guaranteed to go to the World Cup in South Korea.

They just needed one goal. A draw would
be enough.

Early in the game, England had a free kick.
They were David Beckham's speciality,
but he missed with his shot. England then got
another free kick. Beckham stepped up.
And missed again. 🙁

David's 'Events' were his failure to score.
No matter how hard he tried, it seemed England
were destined to fail.

But what was David's response?

Quit? Decide he wasn't going to score that day?

No. He kept trying.

In the final minute, England got another free kick. There was just one minute left. David Beckham had failed to score with his previous two attempts.

What was his response when one of his teammates offered to take the free kick?

Well if he had left it to them and they missed, at least he wouldn't be blamed. But Beckham took responsibility. He believed in himself. He knew he had worked hard practising free kicks.

He stepped up.
Took the free kick.

And scored!

Get in.

Now even if you don't like football, that story about David Beckham is still a great example of

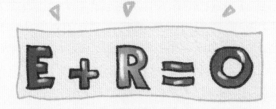

E + R = O

(And if you do enjoy football, go to YouTube and type in England v Greece World Cup Qualifier 2001 to see what I'm talking about.)

Here are a couple of other examples of famous people and their attitudes to events that don't always go well.

I love this quote from the tennis player Serena Williams. She's been incredibly successful, but she's also had her setbacks. When those setbacks happen, what's her 'Response'?

I really think a champion is defined not by their wins but by how they recover when they fall

Serena Williams

'I really think a champion is defined not by their wins but by how they recover when they fall.'

Here's another quote of hers I find inspiring.

'With a defeat, when you lose, you get up . . . you try again. That's what I do in life when I get down, when I get sick, I don't want to just stop. I keep going and I try to do more.'

J. K. Rowling's 'event' was that publishers kept rejecting her proposal for her first Harry Potter book. Her 'Response'? Keep trying! Millions of people around the world are glad she did.

The formula

has been really helpful for me. Without it, you wouldn't be reading this book. Why?

Let me explain.

A few years ago, I wanted to write a book called SUMO, for adults. I was really excited about doing so.

My friend Steve put me in touch with one of the largest publishers in the UK – he had a book published through them and it had sold loads!

I pitched my idea to Steve's publisher. On his advice I wrote one chapter (I worked really hard to make sure it was a great one) and wrote a summary of what the rest of the book was about.

I waited excitedly to hear back from the publisher. Two weeks later they contacted me.

I nervously read the email.

What did they think?

They didn't like my book proposal and they HATED the title SUMO (Shut Up, Move On). I was gutted.

So that was my 'Event'.

What was my 'Response'?

Well, I discovered the lady who had contacted me, called Rachel, was going to be at an event that my mate Steve was speaking at. I had been invited and so had she. My thinking was, if I could meet Rachel face to face, I might be able to persuade her that SUMO would sell well and I had an idea what image we could put on the front cover which would make people think SUMO was fun and a little quirky – but not aggressive. The idea was to have my SUMO logo on the cover – a cartoon SUMO character on a unicycle!

You see I've learnt that sometimes we only properly connect with people when we meet them face to face and can talk to them – rather than always using technology to communicate.

In a world of iPhones and iPads, never forget the importance of **eyeballs**

But how could I have responded to this setback?

Sulked. Moaned to Steve. Given up. Realised it was a stupid idea anyway.

You could say that they would have been valid responses. And if I had responded in those ways what would the '**Outcome**' have been?

No book.

So, I rang up Rachel and asked if we could meet up for a coffee before Steve's event. When I spoke to her, I immediately realised this – she was actually a really nice, friendly person.

This is worth remembering isn't it?

Just because someone doesn't agree with you doesn't mean they dislike you

Rachel agreed to meet me.

Brilliant. This was my chance to use all my persuasive charm.

Unfortunately, it seems my persuasive charm was on holiday that day. Rachel remained unconvinced. A week later she emailed me with what was to be her last contact with me.

Although still friendly, she was also pretty clear.

'A book title has to work from the outset and Paul, yours doesn't.'

Despite my perseverance and positivity, it seemed my outcome would be the same.

No book.

Life can be like that sometimes. We get setbacks and disappointments despite being positive and persevering. When we do, our response still matters. It would have been so tempting just to spend hours sending out invites to my pity party.

What I did instead was ring my good mate, Paul, for some advice.

Paul was helpful and encouraging. He liked my SUMO ideas and felt they could help a lot of people. He gave me a great piece of advice and it's one that I'm sure could help you in the future. It was simply this:

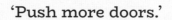

> Push more doors
> because you only need one
> of them to open

Well I had to push a lot of doors. It seemed Rachel was not alone in being unconvinced by the title of my book – even with a SUMO character on a unicycle on the cover.

I had 13 publishers reject it in total. But Paul kept up his encouragement.

'Push more doors.'

One eventually opened and the book came out 27 May 2005. It's since sold over 150,000 copies and has been translated into 11 different languages, including Australian. ☺

The publisher who launched my SUMO book is the same publisher of the one you're reading now. But what if I'd given up? What if I hadn't asked for help from my friend Paul?

S.U.M.O. Challenge

Who can you think of who's maybe famous, who has had some setbacks, but still responded positively? Have you got any examples of when you responded well to a setback?

So that's

$$E + R = O$$

It's a simple formula that can help you to say **YESSS!** to not giving up, to seeing setbacks as stepping stones to your success. It could also help you say **YESSS!** to asking for help from people and to keep pushing on and not giving up. In life we can get good events. But it's still up to us to make the most of them. Sometimes our events are difficult. When this happens, it's easy to give up or look to blame other people for what has happened.

If you do so, you will get an **O**utcome.

But what if it's not the **O**utcome you wanted?

You see, we can't always change the events that happen to us, but we can look at how we respond to them.

It's a magic formula.

When you have events that don't go well, how do you usually respond? How might you respond differently having read about this SUMO Secret?

🎣 Have you ever used the BSE (Blame Someone Else) card? Do you know anyone else who has one of these cards? (Adults use them as well.) I used mine for years, but in the end it wasn't helping me, so I binned it. Permanently.

🎣 When you have some difficult events, how might being in the **Red** Cap part of your brain affect you?

🎣 How interested are you to explore how other responses to events can lead to different and better outcomes for you? If you are, you will find the rest of the SUMO Secrets really useful in helping you to be more positive, confident and able to

say **YESSS!** to so many things in life.

The MOST IMPORTANT PERSON You'll Ever Talk to Is . . .

● ● ●

Have you ever met someone who is really important or

famous

I've met a few famous sports people, and I also met two former Prime Ministers, David Cameron and Theresa May, when I was speaking at a charity event.

Someone I've never met is the Queen. I've heard lots of good things about her, and the other day I was thinking what I would say to her if I did ever meet her.

'How's the family?'

Possibly not.

Maybe I would give her a copy of this book and say: 'This is for your great grandchildren when they get older.'

Any ideas what you would say to her?

'Who's your favourite YouTuber?'

'Have you ever done a Tik Tok video?'

'How many followers have you got on Instagram?'

I think when my kids were younger, they'd have probably asked: 'When you take your dogs for a walk, do you have a plastic bag with you to pick up their poo?'

They may not be famous, but if we're talking about important people, I guess we're going to need to include teachers, aren't we? After all, they can help you learn all kinds of things, and prepare you to do your best in your exams. Sometimes it's a particular teacher or coach who takes time to listen to you and encourage you – wow, that can be really helpful can't it?

Your parents or other adults are also important. They can have a huge influence on you. My Mum has always been a great encourager, and still is today. Sadly, when I was a teenager, my stepfather said and did some pretty awful things. Fortunately, he's not been in my life for a long time. (I guess that also shows that even if you have some bad experiences growing up, it is still possible to make something of your life. What seems like a 'No' period of your life can still develop into a

'  ' life.)

But forget Prime Ministers, members of the royal family, teachers and parents for the moment. This chapter is focusing on someone who, whatever happens, is always going to be with you. Their influence on you is far greater than you may realise, and you're always talking to them and listening to their opinions even when you don't realise it.

Who am I talking about?

I'm talking about you!

Yep, you are an incredibly important and influential person – on yourself!

DO YOU TALK TO YOURSELF?

Actually, you do. Everyone does. As soon as you read the question you had a conversation inside your head. (Some people call that your 'self-talk'. Others call it your 'inner dialogue'.) But one way to describe it is simply this – 'Your Thinking'.

When I'm working with adults, I spend a great deal of time talking about how we think – it's a BIG and really IMPORTANT subject. And I explain why we all need to develop FRUITY THINKING.

Strange name, eh?

I call it that because we know fruit can be good for our bodies, and it provides us with vitamins, but we also need to think about our minds – what's going on inside our heads. Wouldn't it be good for our health if our thinking had the same effect as fruit does on our bodies?

Well it can.

WHAT'S THE BIG DEAL ABOUT HOW YOU THINK?

Let me introduce you to something I find really helpful in understanding the importance of my thinking. I call it the **T.E.A.R.** process.

These are the thoughts or conversations we have inside our heads all the time. In many ways, thinking is a bit like breathing: we are doing it all the time, but we are not always aware that we are, and we don't always realise how our thoughts are affecting us.

Here's something else that's fascinating about our thinking.

When we think, we often think in questions. For example:

'What time is it?'

'What's for tea?'

'How come my mate is so good at everything?'

'What will people think if I ask a question in class?'

'Will I be laughed at for the clothes I'm wearing?'

You'll see later why I've mentioned that we often think in questions.

Now, imagine I get you to think about something that makes you happy. Perhaps it was a party you went to, a sleepover with friends, going to a concert, having a takeaway or going to Nando's. Maybe it's playing video games, scrolling for memes, walking your dog (always easier to do if you have one), or watching a funny video on YouTube.

When you think about some of these things, guess what is also happening? You're affecting your . . .

**motions**, or how you feel. I could also get you to think of some sad things that may have happened and that would also affect your emotions and feelings.

Now, how you feel can also influence your . . .

ctions If I'm feeling happy and positive, I am more likely to behave in a positive way. If I feel confident, I might enjoy trying new things.

However, if I am feeling anxious or nervous, I might be less likely to do things. Which is fine, but it shows the strong relationship between our emotions, our feelings and our actions.

Whatever actions we take, or don't take, ultimately, we will always get . . .

esults Our actions have outcomes. They have consequences.

Let's look at an example of how our **hinking**

can ultimately influence our **esults**.

Imagine you have Maths tomorrow at school. And for this example, let's pretend Maths is not your strongest subject. Let's see what impact your thinking can have on your Maths lesson.

Thinking

I don't enjoy Maths. I'm not very good. Loads of kids in class are far better at it than me. I'm just stupid. The questions are so hard.

Emotions

I feel anxious. What if I'm asked a question and I don't know the answer? I'm feeling demotivated and wishing I was doing something else.

Actions

What's the point of trying? I can't do it. I'll have a laugh with a few of my mates instead. It will wind up the teacher but at least it might impress some of my mates.

Results

I don't learn anything in the lesson. I get a detention for messing around in class. I could be outside having a good time with my friends but I'm not. I'm inside. And I'm still no good at maths.

OK, so that's how T.E.A.R. unfolded in that first scenario. But what if your thinking changed?

I'm not great at Maths. So, I'll really need to concentrate in the lesson. If I don't understand something, I'll need to ask the teacher. I bet some of my mates don't always know the answers either. I just need to make sure that with every lesson I get a bit better at Maths.

I'm a little anxious, but I'm OK. I don't feel stupid because I know that some of my mates find Maths hard too.

 **Actions**

I concentrate in class. I need to understand this. When I don't understand, I'll ask questions or ask the teacher to go through it more slowly with me.

 **Results**

I get to learn something in the lesson. I still don't find it easy and I need to concentrate, but I start to feel quite good. And after a hard Maths lesson, it's good to hang out with my mates over lunch. That beats detention any day. ☺

little **S.U.M.O.** Thought

Your thinking matters massively

It's like when you see a set of dominoes all stood up next to one another. You can have a thousand stacked up in a line, but you only need to push the first one and they will all eventually fall down.

Our thoughts are a little like that first domino. It can impact on everything.

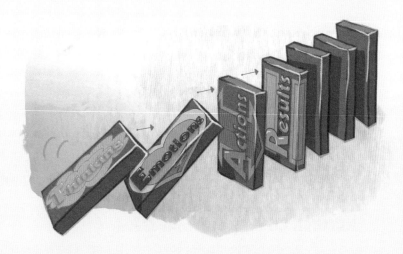

So how we think – the conversations we have inside our heads – are just soooooo important.

Sadly, and without us realising it, both young people and adults don't always think in a way that helps them – sometimes it hurts them.

It's not **that they are experiencing.**

It's **FAULTY THINKING**

'Faulty' means it's not working. It's not giving us the results we want.

That's not good.

LET'S LOOK AT TWO TYPES OF FAULTY THINKING

NUMBER ONE: The Inner Critic

Some people can spend a lot of time being really harsh, beating themselves up with what they say to themselves inside their heads. They may say or think things like:

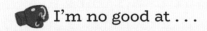 I'm no good at . . .

I'm hopeless at sport

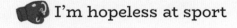 I'm ugly

No one likes me

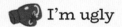 They're really popular – I'm not

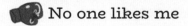 Everyone thinks I'm stupid

I will never get a good job in the future

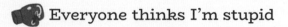 I will never be able to . . .

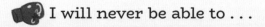 I'm always getting things wrong

I'm not very clever

It's like we go around with an imaginary big red boxing glove and we keep hitting ourselves, often over minor things.

As a result, we aren't happy. We can lack confidence and never take risks because we're thinking 'what if I fail?'

And sometimes we can be really skilled at magnifying things. In other words, we focus on a small mistake, or something we don't like about ourselves, and magnify it into something huge. We can all do that at times, and can get a distorted view of ourselves.

If you're watching a film and press pause, the actors could in that moment have a weird facial expression or their eyes closed. Imagine if they just focused on that one still frame! It's not an accurate representation of themselves though is it?

But we can take one small aspect of our lives or our appearance and focus on it so much and make it a far bigger issue than it really is. And at that point we really need to apply our Blue Cap thinking brain and realise what we're doing. That's why this next section is so important.

What you focus on magnifies

But imagine if it wasn't your Inner Critic's voice you were listening to, but your Inner SUMO Coach instead? You see, your Inner SUMO Coach will have kinder, more helpful conversations with you.

7 THINGS OUR INNER SUMO COACH WILL TELL US

Everyone gets things wrong at times. It's how you learn. You may have come across the following if you've learnt about Growth Mindset: see a **FAIL** as a

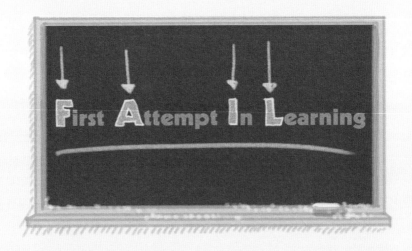

Remember, the most successful person you know has failed in their lives. Believe me they have.

So, here's the deal:
'Failure isn't final until you stop trying'. OK?

And if you're still not convinced that failure is part of life, how about this quote from J. K. Rowling on the topic.

'Some failure in life is inevitable. It is impossible to live without failing at something, unless you live so cautiously that you might as well not have lived at all – in which case you fail by default.'

Hey, maybe you're not the best at everything you do. That's fine. Just focus on getting a little better today than you were yesterday. Focus on progress not perfection.

Compare yourself with who you were yesterday, rather than always comparing yourself with your friends or people on social media.

3 Quit being down on yourself – you're already a winner. Seriously. In order to create you, millions of sperm cells had a race to fertilise an egg. You are you because just one of them won that race! If it hadn't and another one had won, you wouldn't be you!

4 Most people have things they would like to change about themselves. Please don't think you are the only person who has at times not felt good about themselves. We all have.

Yes, even those people who keep posting great pictures of themselves on Instagram. Getting fit and wanting to look good is fine – just remember that it doesn't determine your worth as a person. A new crisp £10 note is not worth more than an old screwed up, dirty one. So celebrate your uniqueness and start appreciating who you are rather than regretting who you aren't.

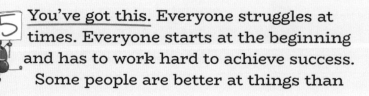

5 You've got this. Everyone struggles at times. Everyone starts at the beginning and has to work hard to achieve success. Some people are better at things than

you because they've practised a lot and had support.
It's not because they are a genius
and you're not.

Successful people apply some **G.R.I.T.**

How about you say to yourself:

Get Ready I'm Trying

We all need to say that phrase to ourselves at times.

It's about saying to trying, to pushing,

to not giving up.

 Guess what? No one is perfect. We all
make mistakes. That's what makes
us human! :)

But when you make a mistake or fail at something, it's not the time to quit and beat yourself up. It's a time to ask:

◼ What can I learn from this?

◼ What will I do differently next time?

◼ Who can I ask for support?

7 Imagine one of your friends is struggling and seems down. Maybe they've split up with their boyfriend or girlfriend. Maybe they have had a big row with their parents, or are just feeling confused about their own feelings or their identity.

They come to you for help.

How would you be with them?

Kind? Caring? Supportive and understanding? What tone of voice would you speak to them in?

Think of things you might say to your friend and write them below:

◼

◼

◼

Have you noticed how supportive and kind we can be to others? How about we treat ourselves like we would treat our best friend? Not with harshness, but with kindness. Not with constant criticism but with some compassion.

Your Inner Coach would say in a very kind, clear and encouraging voice:

Be your own
best friend

I think that's advice worth following, don't you?

Which of those seven Inner SUMO Coach sayings did you like best? Go through all seven and write down some key phrases that it would be good to remind yourself of. Maybe you could write them on a white board or a piece of card and put them somewhere you will see them regularly.

I was once working with a footballer who played in the Premier League. I was talking about the red boxing glove and the dangers of constantly beating yourself up. He told me this . . .

'If I have a bad game, I will beat myself up after the match for an hour or two. But then I say to myself, "Just because you had a bad game, doesn't make you a bad player".'

This person's thinking made him bounce back from a setback, rather than convince himself he was no good. And you can do the same.

Here's the second type of Faulty Thinking.

NUMBER TWO: Victim Thinking

This is <u>IMPORTANT</u>. There are genuine victims in life – victims of crime, victims of abuse and other awful things. This section is <u>not</u> about people who've suffered such things. It's about how all of us at times get into a way of thinking that is not very helpful and prevents us

saying **YESSS!** to life's opportunities.

Here's what I mean by Victim Thinking.

It's when we believe that life is always unfair and that we have little or no control over our lives. What happens to us is simply down to chance, and never due to our own choices.

In Victim Thinking, when things go wrong, we don't look in the mirror and reflect on how our actions or behaviour may have contributed to the situation. We simply reach into our pocket and play the card we looked at in the magic formula chapter

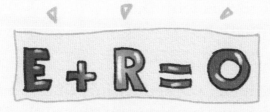

$$E + R = O$$

Remember?

It's our BSE card.

What did BSE stand for again?

Blame Someone Else.

Blame Someone Else
Start Date: Birth
End Date: Never

#NotMyFault
#NothingICanDo

We blame our parents, other adults, our friends, our teachers – we just never think to look at ourselves! It's always someone else's fault. If I'm honest, I think most people have at times played the BSE card. I certainly have.

Remember, when we're in our Red Cap Brain, we can be faced with a challenge and react with either a fight or flight response.

Victim Thinking is our way of fleeing from the situation and not taking responsibility or ownership for how to resolve things.

It's easier to do this – and Red Cap Brain loves taking the easy option – than it is to put on your Blue Cap and think about how to deal with the situation.

I remember a specific time, when I was in Victim Thinking and played the BSE card, although I didn't realise it at the time. (That's the thing to remember – we're not always aware of how our thinking affects our behaviour.)

School was a bit of a rollercoaster for me. I did OK in some subjects (English and Drama) but struggled in many others. I've mentioned some already – Pottery, Physics, Maths, and you can also add Biology to the list too.

Geography was a subject I was OK at, although I didn't enjoy it much. We once went on a Geography field trip to a place called 'Boggle Hole' near Robin Hood's Bay. The name of the place was funny, but I don't think I learnt anything from the trip.

I did three A levels at school, English Literature, History and Geography. My results were pretty good in the first two, but after two years of study I failed Geography A level – which probably put an end to my dreams of ever being a Geography teacher and running a field trip to Boggle Hole! ☺

A few years later, when I was finishing my degree, I went for a job interview with a big company.

I really wanted to work for them and had prepared really well for my interview. Then I was asked a question I wasn't expecting.

'Why do you think you failed Geography A level?'

I wasn't expecting that and so I said the first thing that came to mind – my fast, **Red** Cap Brain sprang into action.

'It was the teachers. They weren't very good. In fact, they were really boring. That's why I failed.'

The interviewer replied:

'Did everyone else who took Geography A level in your class fail as well?'

'Er . . . No, some did OK I think.'

The interviewer then really started to reveal that I was in Victim Thinking with their next question.

'Did they have the same teachers as you?'

'Yes they did,' I replied.

'But they passed and you didn't?'

'ER ... yes.'

The interview was far shorter than I expected. There weren't many more questions after that. Without realising it, I had put all the blame and responsibility for failing my Geography A level on the teachers.

I didn't get the job.

I still think to this day that they weren't the best teachers I've ever had. But let's be realistic – not all teachers are amazing. In fact, whatever job people do, accountant, IT specialist, gardener, fashion designer, doctor, software developer, there will always be some people who are better at what they do than others. FACT.

But I blamed just one group of people for my failure. My teachers. And I never asked myself if I'd tried my hardest

It is so easy to do.

It's easy not to take responsibility. It gets us off the hook. And it can become a habit: something we do on autopilot without thinking.

Well it might be easy to do, but it's not helpful. When you do it, you're basically shouting 'No' to life. 😦

Lots of people can slip into Victim Thinking. If it happens just occasionally then hopefully that won't have too much of an impact. But if seeing yourself as a victim becomes your identity, then it's like your favourite piece of clothing is a T-shirt with the word Victim on it. By wearing it constantly, you're telling yourself and others how you see yourself.

What are the long-term consequences of seeing yourself as a victim when you believe you have no control over your life whatsoever?

HERE'S THREE POSSIBLE ONES:

Ⓥ You might not fulfil your potential. You give up too easily when setbacks happen because you just don't think you can succeed and are not as lucky as other people.

Ⓥ You miss out on opportunities. You're so busy feeling sorry for yourself because one door has closed that you fail to spot there are other doors to push.

Ⓥ Other people miss out on your unique abilities because you failed to develop and become the person you could have been. 😦 😦 😦

When you wear the Victim T-shirt, you become a passenger in your life and allow circumstances and other people to determine your 'destination' and that is NOT saying **YESSS!** to life 😞

Let's look at some Victim sayings but then contrast
them with some SUMO sayings.

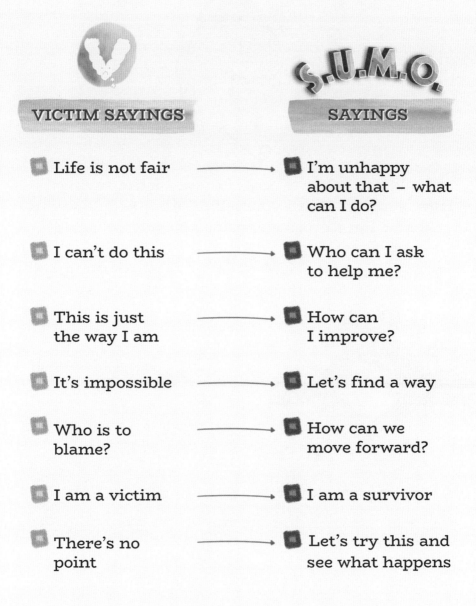

VICTIM SAYINGS	SAYINGS
Life is not fair	I'm unhappy about that – what can I do?
I can't do this	Who can I ask to help me?
This is just the way I am	How can I improve?
It's impossible	Let's find a way
Who is to blame?	How can we move forward?
I am a victim	I am a survivor
There's no point	Let's try this and see what happens

Could you relate to any of those Victim sayings? Have you ever heard yourself or other people saying them? Put a cross alongside any you have said.

Which one of the S.U.M.O. sayings did you like?

S.U.M.O. Challenge

How about you make a card or poster with a positive SUMO message on it or make a design for a T-shirt with your own SUMO saying on it. You could come up with your own slogan and logo. I would love it if you could post a picture of it on Instagram and tag me in @theSumoguy #theSumosecrets. Not only would I be thrilled to see what you've designed, but your message could be an inspiration to other young people.

Slipping into Victim Thinking is easy for us all to do at times. The key to change is to become aware that you are doing it and the consequences of staying in that kind of thinking.

Because remember, your **Thinking** influences your **Emotions**, that impact on your **Actions**, that lead to **Results**.

(**T.E.A.R.**). So changing our Thinking is really important if we want to get better results in life.

Let me finish this SUMO Secret by giving you a gift.

Well it's not really a gift, more a toolbox. I know adults have found the following really helpful, and I reckon you will too.

We learnt earlier that people sometimes think in questions. I've developed seven questions that (when you realise you've been spending too long listening to your Inner Critic, or have put on that Victim T-shirt and slipped into Victim Thinking) can help you move into Fruity Thinking.

They are like vitamins for your mind. They help you when you are in Red Cap Brain 🎩 to also use your Blue Cap Brain 🧢. I wonder which ones you'll find especially helpful?

They're really good questions to ask when you've had a problem or setback in life.

HERE THEY ARE:

1. Where is this issue on a scale of 1–10 (where 10 = death or the end of the world)?

2. How important will it be in one week's time?

3. Is my response appropriate and effective?

4. How can I influence or improve the situation?

5. What can I learn from this?

6. What would I do differently next time?

7. What can I find that's positive in the situation?

Below is a postcard image that we have for adults.
The questions are almost exactly the same –
except for one of them.

After you've spotted which one it is, think of the reason why the one for younger people is slightly different from the one for adults?
You can download this postcard from my website www.thesumoguy.com or email yesss@thesumoguy.com and we'll send you the link. If you're feeling creative you could always design your own seven questions card – and remember, if you do, I would love to see what you come up with (@theSumoguy #theSumosecrets). ☺

There have been a lot of important things to think about in this SUMO Secret – but the key thing to remember is. . .

The most important person You will ever talk to is YOU!

So listen to your Inner SUMO Coach  a lot more from now on and be careful what the message is you're wearing on your T-shirt.

BLUE CAP BRAIN REFLECTION TIME

Which one of the two types of

Faulty Thinking _____ did you relate to most, the Inner Critic or Victim Thinking? Or did you relate to both of them?

When you're in that type of thinking, how does it affect you?

What will you do to make sure you remember the Inner SUMO Coach sayings that are really important to you?

Which of those seven questions on the postcard did you like? In what situations could you see yourself using them?

S.U.M.O. Secret 4

Hippos Do It And So Should You

When my children were young, they used to enjoy dressing up and playing games like 'Let's pretend'.

We have a picture of my son Matt pretending to be a doctor when he was 3, complete with a stethoscope around his neck. And all these years later, he actually is a doctor.

Amazing eh?

My daughter Ruth used to dress up as Snow White, but so far there's no sign that she's set up home with the Seven Dwarfs since she started her job in London.

As we get older, we can still pretend. It's unlikely we dress up (although some people do) but we can still pretend to be happy when actually we're not. That isn't helpful though. You see, it's good to be honest with ourselves, and also with other people, about how we're feeling.

Why?

Well if I hurt my leg (which I did recently when out jogging) it's not good to pretend that I'm OK. Because if I do, I'm not getting the support or treatment I need to help me recover.

Now it's great when we're happy and feeling good, but let's be really clear – it's not wrong to feel unhappy sometimes.

little S.U.M.O. Thought

It's OK to not always feel OK

In our teenage years, lots of things are changing for us physically. We're growing up. Hormones, those chemical substances our body produces, are impacting our physical development and our moods. Parents and adults around us can seem annoying – even more so than previously! We can also add into the mix the fact that secondary school brings lots of changes too. Many can be really positive:

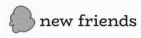 new friends

 new teachers

 new subjects to study

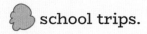 school trips.

But it can bring changes that might not always be as positive to begin with:

You may find schoolwork a lot harder.

Some of your mates may be more physically mature than you – and you may get picked on as a result.

You may have to travel further to school, and your day could seem so much longer.

Despite needing more sleep as a teenager, you may have to get up even earlier!

There's so much more homework too!

You feel under more pressure from your peers.

When you're experiencing so many changes, your emotions and feelings can seem like they're the counter in a game of Snakes and Ladders. Some squares you land on are OK and not much happens. Some squares you land on are ladders ☺ but some squares are snakes. ☹

Life can be a bit like the snakes and ladders game sometimes – it can be full of ups and downs. And remember it's the same for adults too, and sometimes adults find it hard to support children when they are having to deal with their own snakes.

But I know what you're wondering.

OK Paul, I understand I'm experiencing a lot of changes as I grow up – and I get that life can be like a game of Snakes and Ladders but. . .

. . . where do the hippos come in? Are they playing Snakes and Ladders too?

I'm glad you asked!

One of the SUMO ideas I talk about with adults is 'Hippo Time is OK'. You see, hippos like to wallow. They roll about in the mud.

Sometimes people need a wallow too. No, I don't mean find the nearest mud bath, get your swimming gear on and dive straight in (although it probably sounds more fun than English homework). But just as hippos go into the mud to get out of the heat and cool down, we might also need to do the same – to give ourselves some time out to 'cool down' and allow ourselves some 'Hippo Time'. And just as being in the mud and water protects a hippo's skin from the effects of too much sun, we need to care for ourselves too, especially our emotions.

Here's one way to view Hippo Time:

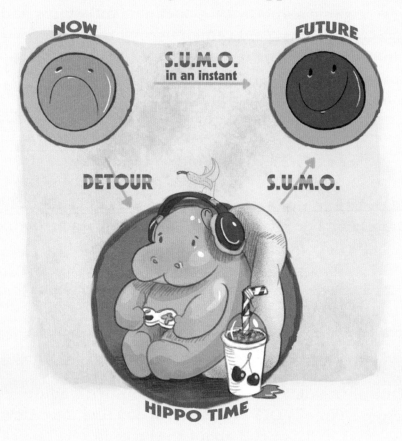

Let's explore this diagram.

There are times when things don't go as we wanted,
but we recover quickly. We feel down for hardly any
time at all. It's easy to SUMO . . . in other words, not
get down for too long and quickly move on. Maybe
you lost a game you were playing with a friend,
but you immediately start playing a new game and
quickly get over your disappointment.

Can you think of a time when that happened to you?

But that won't always be the case. You and I are not robots or machines. We can't turn our emotions on and off at the flick of a switch. Unfortunately, we can't bubble-wrap our feelings and protect them from ever being hurt. We might like to, but that isn't an option.

So there will be times when just like in the game of Snakes and Ladders, we'll land on a snake. That's why . . .

IT'S OK TO FEEL MAD, BAD OR SAD SOMETIMES

Some young people when they feel this way believe that something is really wrong with them and that they shouldn't be having those feelings. Here's a lie we might believe:

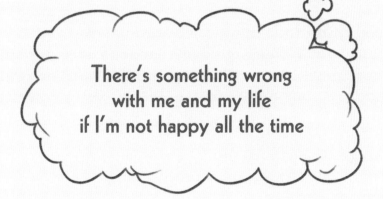

There's something wrong with me and my life if I'm not happy all the time

That's not a helpful belief. In fact, look at the word 'belief'. One way to write the word is be**LIE**f.

So, it's really important you remember the following:

Don't believe everything you think

If you think that there's something wrong with you because you're feeling angry, anxious or sad, realise those negative emotions are normal and helpful. They are your body's way of letting you know that not everything is right.

You could see your emotions as a bit like your internal smoke alarm.

Let me explain.

Sometimes the smoke alarm goes off in our house unnecessarily – the toast is only slightly burnt. We can be like that sometimes, getting upset over something that's not really that important. But what you don't want to do is ignore the smoke alarm or, even worse, remove its batteries. Likewise, it's important you don't ignore your emotions and feelings, because they are giving you some information that you might need to act on.

That's why Hippo Time is so important, because it gives you permission and time to acknowledge and process how you're feeling.

Now you might need Hippo Time for all kinds of reasons, but what causes you to need some could be different from other people. I need some Hippo Time when my favourite football teams Wigan Athletic and Bradford City lose. And that happens a lot. But unless you support either of these teams you won't feel like I do most Saturday nights!

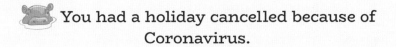

REASONS WHY YOU MIGHT NEED HIPPO TIME . . .

You had a holiday cancelled because of Coronavirus.

You breakup from a really special relationship with someone.

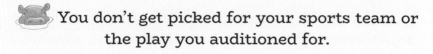 You forget your PE kit and you love PE.

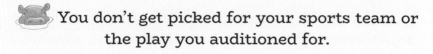 You don't get picked for your sports team or the play you auditioned for.

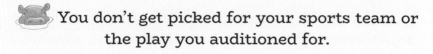 You move house and don't see your friends as much.

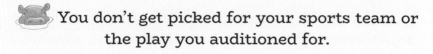 An adult stops you doing something you really want to do.

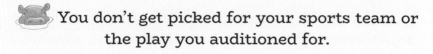 Your PlayStation won't work.

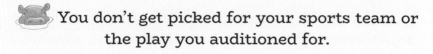 You are getting bullied at school.

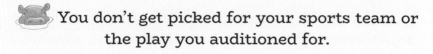 You have an argument with your parents.

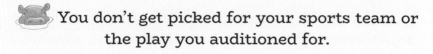 You're struggling with your identity and are feeling confused.

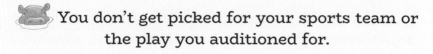 Your parents separate.

 Your favourite band splits up.

What other things can you think of that might mean you need a little Hippo Time? (Think of two others for you.)

Which part of your brain are you in when you're in Hippo Time – your Red or Blue Cap?

The answer?

You're definitely in your 🎩 Red Cap part of your brain, which is the emotional part of your brain. And that's OK, it's normal.

Just remember, the 🧢 Blue Cap part of your brain is where you do your logical, rational thinking – so when you're in Hippo Time, it is easy for all of us (including me) to become irrational about how we're feeling, and even exaggerate things some of the time.

That's especially the case when you're a teenager. Your emotions can feel intensified due to all the changes going on in your brain. Your internal smoke alarm can be triggered by something quite small, but you might see everything as a major catastrophe.

WHEN WE BELIEVE SOMETHING REALLY BAD HAS HAPPENED, WE MIGHT START THINKING:

 I will always feel this way.

My life will never be happy again.

 There is no hope.

And if we start thinking this way and believing it (remember, some beliefs can actually be lies) we start to feel even worse. So, our feelings and emotions can become even more intense. It's like we start to slip deeper and deeper into the mud, and when that happens it becomes harder to move out of Hippo Time.

IMPORTANT POINT: HERE'S WHAT'S GOOD TO REMEMBER ABOUT YOUR FEELINGS

Feelings can fade over time. How you feel about something today might not be how you feel about that same thing in a few hours, a few days or a few weeks.

Feelings can be like clouds in the sky. You see them, they are real, but eventually they pass by.

Most feelings of hurt, sadness or anger are like bruises not tattoos. They are not permanent and eventually they fade away. (Although sometimes we might need help from others to recover.)

SO WHAT HELPFUL THINGS CAN YOU DO WHEN YOU NEED SOME HIPPO TIME?

Remember, we are all different; so these are some suggestions, not rules!

 1 Accept you need Hippo Time – it's OK! Remember, negative emotions are normal, healthy and often helpful.

2 Try and label how you feel, if you can, and say it out loud to yourself. For example: 'I'm feeling hurt at the moment.' (This will make you feel clearer and less confused about how you're feeling, and help you access the Blue Cap part of your brain.) Be careful, though, of what words you use to describe your feelings. It might be more helpful to say 'I'm currently feeling low' rather than 'I'm depressed'.

Hippo Time is OK!

little S.U.M.O. Thought

Remember your feelings are what you're experiencing – they're not your identity

3 Give yourself some time and space to digest how you're feeling. Your body needs time to digest its food. You need time to digest your feelings. You're not removing the batteries from your internal smoke alarm, you're taking time to understand why you're feeling the way you are. You're accepting your feelings, not denying them.

A good question you might want to ask yourself is: 'I wonder why I'm feeling this way?' You may come up with more than one reason, or perhaps none at all. There's no pressure to come up with a reason, but at least give yourself the time to explore what could be causing you to feel the way you do.

WARNING

While it can be helpful to spend some time on your own during Hippo Time, be careful you don't become isolated and withdraw from people. It's good to talk things through with other people and get their support and also their perspective. Often you will feel much better after you've done so.

4 Play a favourite game, or song, or both. Distraction can be helpful and can help lift your mood. Music can be like a massage for your emotions.

5 Go on YouTube and watch some videos that make you smile. Here's one I recommend – go to YouTube and type in 'Hippo fart sounds like a chainsaw'. ☺☺☺

6 Plan something you'll look forward to doing – seeing friends, going to the cinema, having some of your favourite food. If you're struggling to come up with ideas, think about when you've had a great day. What did you do? Who did you see?

Here's a phrase I use a lot with people I work with:

Don't hope for happy times **PLAN THEM**

It's good to have something to look forward to even if we don't feel great at the moment. This will appeal to your Red Cap Brain, which seeks out ways to make you happy.

7 Write a poem, a song, a rap, or a letter to express how you're currently feeling. Or you could draw or paint a picture. Remember, if you prefer to keep it private, whatever you write, draw or paint can be for your eyes only. But whatever you do could be a helpful release for the emotions you're experiencing.

8 Go to bed earlier. Sleep is so good for you. (Even more so than pizza!) Our brains are busy working and processing the day's events while we're snoozing. That's why we can feel better about things after a good night's sleep.

Now if someone says you're sleeping too much, you could reply 'Chill out guys I'm just allowing my brain to carry out some essential maintenance and repairs'. ☺

 Take some kind of exercise. Which of these could you do?

Where would you place your tick?

	NO WAY	POSSIBLY	YES DEFINITELY
Go for a run	☐	☐	☐
Go for a bike ride	☐	☐	☐
Play in the park with friends	☐	☐	☐
Go to the gym	☐	☐	☐
Go for a swim	☐	☐	☐
Go for a long walk	☐	☐	☐
Play football	☐	☐	☐
Dance along to a song	☐	☐	☐

What else could you do? _____

It's important we remember this:

**Exercise can energise
you and make
you feel better**

But what if you hate exercise? What if you hate
exercise as much as I hate DIY or tidying the garage?
If that's you, no worries. But here is what
is important.

We need to be kind to ourselves, to our bodies,
and to our emotions, especially when we're
having some Hippo Time. And although you
might not realise this, our bodies like being
outside in nature.

Being inside for too long is not good for us. So,
if possible, get outside, get some sunlight, even
when it's not sunny. Notice nature. Stare at a
tree. Notice its leaves and how they move in
the wind. I'm not saying do vigorous exercise
necessarily (although if you do already, that's
a bonus). Just remember, your body likes to
move – it's good for you. So please look
after it – it's the only one you've got!

The main exercise I do is walk. I often put my headphones in and listen to a podcast or music. Sometimes I don't wear headphones but just enjoy the sights and sounds around me. It's like I'm giving my emotions a long hot shower or a lazy relaxing bath.

10 Come up with your '**Thankful Four List**'. Despite how you might be feeling, remember there are always things to be thankful about. Think of four specific things you are grateful for. Maybe it was time with a friend, a meal you had, a programme you watched, or playing with your cat or dog. The key is to be specific about the good things you have experienced.

S.U.M.O. Challenge

Why don't you try that now? List four things about today that you are thankful for:

i.

ii.

iii.

iv.

HERE'S TWO FINAL THINGS YOU MIGHT WANT TO DO WHEN YOU'RE IN HIPPO TIME:

11 Do something nice for someone else. They'll feel good and, surprisingly, so will you! You might offer to do something to help in the house, or help your brother or sister or a friend, or offer to take the dog for a walk – if you have one ☺.

Think about how you feel when you buy someone a gift that they really love – it feels good, doesn't it? Well guess what? You can repeat that feeling when you show kindness to others.

little **S.U.M.O. Thought**

Showing kindness to others
makes you feel better
about yourself

12 If you need to cry, cry. It's OK. Crying can have a soothing effect and can help you feel calmer. Shedding tears releases the brain chemical oxytocin and endorphins, which can ease pain and can make you feel better.

Crying can also be a way of letting others know you need support. And getting support from others rather than struggling on your own is always a good thing.

Social media can be great, but checking out friends' photos on Instagram might not be the best thing for you right now. A photograph is just a snapshot of someone's life. It's not the whole story. But we can all have a tendency at times to compare our unedited lives with the edited highlights of other people's.

Remember, most people only post the best bits of their lives on social media – but if we're emotionally a little fragile, and feeling low, we can end up believing everyone else has a great life and therefore feel worse about our own.

So please remember this.

Don't scroll inside
Take a stroll outside

Snakes, Ladders, and Hippos. . .

Remember that game of Snakes and Ladders we looked at earlier? Well imagine if the game contained no snakes, only ladders. It might feel fun to win at first. Winning would be easy. There would be no challenges or setbacks. Great.

But do you know what?

It would soon become boring, wouldn't it?

We need challenges to grow, just like plants need sunshine and water.

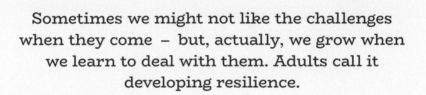

Sometimes we might not like the challenges when they come – but, actually, we grow when we learn to deal with them. Adults call it developing resilience.

Life does have 'snakes' – setbacks and disappointments – but when you land on one, remember it's not the end of the game. You see, the fact is, we all land on snakes at times – even when you might feel it's only you that does.

So when you have a setback, or land on a snake, allow yourself some Hippo Time to wallow, but then pick up the dice and roll again. You will never land on a ladder by giving up – you only land on one when you decide to keep playing the game.

Hippo Time is OK – but remember, it's temporary!

Hippo Time is not meant to last forever. It's part of your journey, but it's not your destination unless you decide to remain there.

MOVE ON

THIS IS IMPORTANT

We can all feel down or low at times – that means everyone, including me! What you have learnt in this chapter will be helpful, but sometimes no matter what we do, we still feel down and low. When that happens, make sure you chat to an adult. You may need some more help. And that's OK. Just make sure you ask for it, and please, whatever you are feeling, remember this:

BE KIND TO YOURSELF.

BLUE CAP BRAIN REFLECTION TIME.

 How easy did you find it to adjust to going to secondary school when you went? What did you enjoy most? What were your challenges?

 What are some of your 'snakes', those things that result in you needing some Hippo Time? Have a look back at the list from pages 83–84 as a reminder.

 Go back to page 87. Out of the twelve things you could do when you're in Hippo Time, choose three that you think you are most likely to help you.

1

2

3

Were there any ideas on that list you had never thought of doing before?

S.U.M.O. Challenge

How do you feel about making a sign that you put on your bedroom door – 'Having Hippo Time. Back soon.'

If you do, I would love to see a picture!
Instagram @theSumoguy #theSumosecrets

S.U.M.O. Secret 5

Don't Forget Your Beachball

Do you enjoy music? My daughter Ruth loves it. When she was a child, we couldn't go anywhere in the car without playing music on the radio or on a cassette tape. (You remember those things don't you? We talked about them briefly in The Magic Formula chapter when we learnt about

$$E + R = O$$)

My son Matt plays the guitar. He's a really good player, but then I would say that, as I'm his Dad. The only musical instrument I've ever played is the recorder – I know how to play the opening line of 'Three Blind Mice'. I never mastered the second line though, and I think in many ways my mum remains slightly disappointed that my musical career never took off.

So it's fair to say, playing a musical instrument isn't my strong point. But I'll tell you what is.

I'm pretty good at blowing up beachballs and then deflating them in record time.

So to the question 'Do you play a musical instrument?' I reply:

'Kind of. If you ever need anyone to play the opening line of "Three Blind Mice" at a party, I'm your man.

Oh, and as an added bonus, I'm really good at blowing up beachballs.'

So how and perhaps more importantly *why* have I developed this skill with beachballs?

OK, I'll tell you. The mystery shall be revealed.

When I'm speaking at events, I'll sometimes ask my audience if they ever have arguments with other people and end up falling out.

And their answer is?

Yep, you're right. Of course they do. Just like young people, adults argue and fall out with each other. It could be their friends, people they work with, even members of their own family. And maybe there are times when they end up falling out with you – although hopefully not for too long.

I wonder if you've ever fallen out with your parents or some of the adults in your life? What about your friends? When I was a teenager, I certainly did.

And although I can still fall out with people now, it happens a lot less than it used to.

And the reason for that?

It's all to do with my beachball.

Let me explain . . .

Imagine you and a friend are both in the same room, but you can't see each other because right in the centre of the room is a ginormous beachball, and you are standing at opposite sides of it.

Although you can't see each other, you can fortunately hear each other.

Then over a loudspeaker a question is asked:

'Please tell me the colour of the beachball.'

You answer immediately: 'Blue, white, and green.'

But your friend answers: 'No it's not, it's red, yellow, and orange.'

So why do you say it's blue, white, and green?

Because from where you are standing, they are the only colours you can see.

And because the beachball is so big and fills the room, you can't see what the other side looks like. Your friend can't see your side though, so they answer with the colours they can see – red, yellow, and orange.

So, which of you has the right answer to the question, you or your friend? Well, if you can't see the other side of the beach ball and can only see blue, white and green, then you will insist you're right.

But if your friend doesn't see those colours, they will think you're wrong. How can it be blue, white, and green when they can clearly see it's red, yellow, and orange?

Life can be a bit like that you know. We see our side of the beachball and automatically think how we see things is right, and if people see things differently from us, they must be wrong.

Ever thought that?

But imagine if we had a drone that could fly above the beachball and see all sides. From the drone's perspective, looking down at the beachball, it would see all six colours, blue, white, green, red, yellow, and orange.

Now the beachball is a really simple visual metaphor to illustrate how life can be at times, and why it is that although two people, or two groups, or even two countries, can be looking at the same thing, 'the beachball', they can see it in very different ways. This can cause all kinds of problems and result in people falling out, arguing and even fighting.

HERE'S WHY.

1. People can believe the colours that they see are the only colours.

2. People may see different colours from each other and believe they can't both be right, one of them has to be wrong – and it's not them!

3. People can be unwilling to explore someone else's perspective – their side of the beachball.

Remember, when you're in the Red Cap part of your brain – the fast brain – you make quick decisions and can jump to conclusions, so you're more likely to see three colours of the beachball and think you have the whole picture. It's only when you slow down and apply the brakes to your thinking and remember your Blue Cap that you start to explore other options.

SO LET'S EXPLORE SOME REASONS WHY PEOPLE MIGHT SEE THE BEACHBALL DIFFERENTLY FROM EACH OTHER

Here are three reasons why people see the beachball (life) differently . . . although there's loads more!

 Adult/teenager perspectives.

If you find an abandoned skateboard while out at the park and take it back to your Gran's, you might be excited about using it. It's unlikely, unless you've got the coolest Gran on the planet, that she is going to say 'Hey you, I want to use it first'. (Although if you do have a picture of your Gran on a skateboard, tag me in on Instagram @theSumoguy #theSumosecrets.)

Your Gran's perspective could be that she's concerned about where you got the skateboard from, and worried that if you use it without protective pads or a helmet you might hurt yourself.

Your view of the 'beachball' is that you've found a skateboard and want to use it and have some fun. But adults looking at the same situation could have a different perspective.

And here's the key

Neither view on finding the skateboard is wrong – they are just different.

Now lots of the people in your world are older than you and may see things differently from you.

You may see the fact that they don't want you to do something as boring, as if they are trying to stop you having fun.

However, they're just thinking 'I don't want you to hurt yourself'.

Or . . . let's imagine you want to stay out late at a friend's house but the adults in your life want you back at a certain time. From their perspective, they don't want you back late as they know you will be tired the next day and that makes you grumpy and moody. They are also thinking you need to be wide awake and alert if you are going to learn anything at school the next day.

Your perspective could be that this adult is head of the fun police and is being deliberately difficult.

But from the adult's side of the beachball, they want you back earlier, not because they're being difficult, but because they care about you.

Interesting hey?

Here's another reason why we see the beachball (life) differently.

 We like different things.

When I was 11 and in my first year at secondary school, I sat next to a boy called Kaushik. We got on really well. For his birthday, he invited me to watch his favourite football team, Manchester United, with his Dad.

I was the only person from the class he invited.

I was THRILLED!!

I love football and I was so excited about seeing Manchester United and going to Old Trafford.

But what if I was a Liverpool supporter?

What if I hated football?

Suddenly my friend Kaushik's kind invitation might be viewed differently by me. I might be thinking 'Can't we go to the cinema instead?' (As it happened, sadly, my stepdad wouldn't allow me to go to the match and I was seriously gutted.)

HERE'S SOMETHING REALLY IMPORTANT TO REMEMBER

People like lots of different things. We can be like each other to look at – most of us have two eyes, a nose and a mouth – and we can be similar ages, but inside we can be quite different.

For instance, here's a list of foods. I bet there's some you like that your friends like also. But I wonder if there's any you enjoy that they don't?

Put a tick alongside the ones you like.

ice cream

broccoli

carrots

chips

burgers (meat or vegetarian)

tacos

curry

milk (from a cow)

hummus

scrambled eggs

ketchup

Yorkshire puddings

chocolate cake

mayonnaise

fish

pineapple

bananas

☐ blue cheese   ☐ strawberries

☐ avocado   ☐ omelettes

☐ Nutella   ☐ sushi

☐ Coke   ☐ samosas

☐ Pepsi   ☐ noodles

☐ tomatoes   ☐ dim sum

If your favourite food wasn't listed, write it here _____

Now choose your favourite five from the list:

1.

2.

3.

4.

5.

If you got your friends to choose their top five, do you think there would be some differences? If you have brothers or sisters, would they choose different ones than you?

My daughter Ruth loves scrambled eggs, omelettes, and Yorkshire puddings, and she used to have ketchup with everything – including Christmas dinner!!

If you gave me omelette or scrambled egg, I'd be asking for the sick bucket!!

So let's appreciate and recognise that we sometimes like different things from each other – and that's OK.

Here's another reason why we may see the beachball differently.

 Our personality.

Some people are very extroverted. They enjoy being with lots of people. When they get home having been with their friends, they are buzzing.

Some people are more introverted. They can enjoy being with their friends but if they have spent a lot of time with people and have not had much time on their own, they can feel tired. If their friends want to see them the next night, they might decide to say no – which doesn't mean they are unfriendly or boring, it just means they might want and need some quiet time on their own, relaxing.

Extroverts may enjoy having lots of friends and spending lots of time with them. Introverts may also have lots of friends and enjoy seeing them just as much – but they'll also enjoy being by themselves sometimes.

So when a school residential trip is organised, an extrovert's side of the beachball might be 'Great I get to spend lots of time with my friends'.

An introvert may also be looking forward to the trip, but not necessarily to having to spend so much time with lots of other people.

little S.U.M.O. Thought

Sometimes people's views aren't right or wrong – just different

There are lots of other reasons why we see 'the beachball' or a situation differently from each other. They also include our upbringing, how much we've travelled, our religious and cultural background, and whether our families have lots of money or very little.

So here are some tips to help you build better relationships with others. You might want to make sure adults see this list too, because it's so easy to see only your side of the beachball, and that isn't always helpful.

SUMO TIPS FOR GETTING ON BETTER WITH OTHERS

1 Remember people see some things differently from you – and that's OK.

2 Ask yourself 'I wonder why they see things that way?' (What's going on in their world that's influencing their perspective?)

3 Listen to what other people have to say, rather than interrupt (adults need to remember this too).

4 Avoid telling people they are wrong. That makes them defensive and less likely to want to listen to you.

5 Don't assume people understand your side of the beachball; sometimes they won't unless you explain it to them.

6 Accept we won't agree on everything, but we can still choose to be kind to each other.

S.U.M.O. Challenge

Talk to your friends, teachers and adults about the beachball. The more people understand this idea, the more likely we are to get along better.

COMMUNICATING YOUR SIDE
OF THE BEACHBALL TO OTHERS

In all my research for this book, one thing has become clear.

Teenagers often don't feel listened to

In other words, adults are good at seeing their side of the beachball, but not always good at seeing yours.

I think the next point is something adults need to be aware of . . .

Adults can be good at talking — but not always good at listening!

So if you have adults in your world who are good at listening to you, that's something to be really positive about.

Either way, here's an idea to improve communication between yourself and some older people in your life. (Remember, it's likely you were given this book by someone older than you, so hopefully they will expect you to want to discuss and even act on some ideas you've read.)

So here goes . . .

How about you write/type/message a note to one or more of the adults in your life, communicating your side of the beachball to them? Now depending on what you want to say, I know this could be really difficult. Talking about things with others can be really hard at times. But it could also be really helpful.

I'm not going to tell you what to write, that's entirely up to you, but here're some phrases to reflect on that might help you decide what to communicate. You could call your message 'From my side of the beachball' – just make sure the person you're writing to understands the concept of the beachball!

From my side of the beach ball . . .

◻ Sometimes I feel . . .

◻ I'd like you to know that . . .

◻ It's not always easy when . . .

◻ I'm sorry that . . .

◼ I really value . . .

◼ What would really help me sometimes is . . .

◼ I'm thankful that . . .

◼ This is hard for me but . . .

Remember, these are just possible phrases you might use. Feel free to use all, some or none of them!

Just be aware that people don't always see your side of the beachball as clearly as you do. Doing this exercise, whether writing a note, sending a text or email, or using it as a way to have a conversation can be really helpful. (If you do this, myself and my team would love to hear how you got on. Please email us at yesss@thesumoguy.com or leave a message on Instagram @theSumoguy #theSumosecrets.)

So that's SUMO Secret number five. Saying to life is so much easier when we get on better with others, and hopefully this secret will help you do that. Relationships can be hard at times, but if we remember our beachball they can always improve.

Which is probably more than I can say for my ability to play the recorder. ☺

BLUE CAP BRAIN REFLECTION TIME

 Have there been situations in your life when you realise you only saw your side of the beachball? What were the consequences?

 How helpful would it be to stop and think about other people's perspective? Is there a personal situation where you realise you've never really thought about their side of the beachball? What could you do to change that?

 How well do you feel other people understand your perspective at times? What could you do to help them be more aware of how you see things?

 Who could you talk to about what you've learnt in this chapter?

S.U.M.O. Secret 6

Making The Magic Happen

So we've reached the last of our SUMO Secrets. Congratulations on making it to this point. I'm really excited about this final secret as it's all about learning to take action to achieve our goals and to make sure we're saying **YESSS!** to life.

However, before we unlock this secret, let's start with a quick quiz.

Below are seven statements. Read the statements and put a score of either 1, 2, or 3 in the box that best describes your response to them. For instance, for statement number one:

'I often **struggle to get motivated to do things**'

If you feel this describes how you are some of the time, then write number 2 in the middle box. After you've responded to all seven statements, count up your scores.

Your final score is simply an indication of how you see yourself at the moment. It's like you're holding up a mirror in front of you in order to see yourself more clearly. The scores are not a reflection of your intelligence in any way. The statements are simply a way to get you thinking about what helps or hinders your ability to make the magic happen.

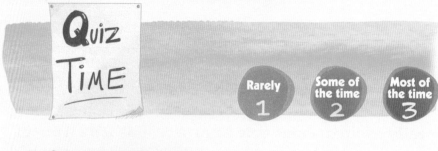

QUIZ **T**IME

	Rarely 1	Some of the time 2	Most of the time 3
1. I often struggle to get motivated to do things	☐	☐	☐
2. I feel overwhelmed at times with the amount of work I have to do	☐	☐	☐

	Rarely 1	Some of the time 2	Most of the time 3
3. If I try something and don't succeed straight away, I can be very hard on myself	☐	☐	☐
4. I get nervous when trying something for the first time	☐	☐	☐
5. I often put off doing things until the last minute	☐	☐	☐
6. If I'm finding something hard to do, I often give up and stop trying	☐	☐	☐
7. I get easily discouraged when I don't see quick results from my work	☐	☐	☐
TOTAL	☐ +	☐ +	☐

GRAND TOTAL =

Key

7 – 11 Do you want to write this chapter? Seriously, based on your score, there are really positive signs that you are already applying many of the SUMO Secrets that will help you in 'making the magic happen'.

12 – 17

This is encouraging! And the good news is you'll gain even more ideas in this chapter to help your progress.

Over 17

Thanks for your honesty. You'll love this chapter. You'll find it of great value in learning how to make your magic happen.

HOW TO MAKE THE MAGIC HAPPEN

Do you ever wonder about what you want to be when you grow up?

My 7% in a Physics exam in Year 10 put paid to any ambitions I had to be a nuclear physicist sadly ☺. A primary school teacher I know asked her class of 4–5 year-olds what they wanted to be when they grew up. The answers included firefighter, nurse, famous, a singer, a zookeeper. The answer that made her smile most though was from the boy who said . . .

'When I grow up, I want to be a rabbit.' ☺

Well I'm all for pursuing your dreams, but that one seems a stretch to me.

However, whatever our goals and plans are, either for now or for the future, one key thing needs to happen for them to become reality . . .

We need to take action.

My friend Ted used to say:

'If you want to experience "satisfaction", take note of the last six letters of the word . . .

Satisf**ACTION**

Everyone has dreams. But dreams are not enough. Success doesn't happen simply because you have a dream or a good idea – it comes about because you did something to achieve it.

A great example of that would be Greta Thunberg and how she has galvanised young people around the world to challenge governments and businesses to take climate change seriously and to protect our planet.

Greta Thunberg

"You must take action. You must do the impossible. Because giving up can never ever be an option."

So why is it that young people and adults want something but don't always take the action needed to achieve it?

What is it that leads to some people thinking about saying **YESSS!** to life, but then not doing anything about it?

There's probably lots of reasons, but we'll take a look at three of them.

THREE REASONS WHY PEOPLE DON'T TAKE ACTION

1. 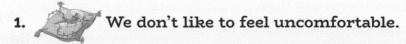 We don't like to feel uncomfortable.

OK, I'd like you to do an experiment with me. If you're able to, stretch both hands out in front of you and clasp them together so that your fingers are intertwined and one thumb is on top of the other. Now, notice which thumb is on top, your left or your right?

When I do it, it's my right thumb that's on top.

Now, separate your hands out again and when you bring them together this time, whichever thumb was on the bottom last time (which would have been my left), put that on the top this time.

How does that feel?

When I do this exercise with the audiences that I'm working with, most of them say it feels strange. It feels different. That's quite often how things can feel in life. Starting a new school, trying a new sport, going to new places, meeting new people – it can be very exciting, but it can also feel different, just like when you change which thumb is on top.

Some people love trying new things, but most people can feel a little nervous to begin with.

Why?

Well our **Red** Cap Brain can make us feel a little anxious at times. Remember: **Red** Cap Brain wants to protect us, so it likes things that are familiar. This part of our brain likes us to feel comfortable. So when we're going to new places or trying something for the first time and we don't know what to expect, it can cause us to feel a little nervous.

And that's OK.

My daughter Ruth is starting a new job in event management in London. Is she excited? Yes. Is she also nervous? Yes. But will she settle into the job and become less nervous? Yes.

However, some people never like to feel uncomfortable, and so they try to avoid doing anything that makes them feel nervous.

Always remember –
nerves are NORMAL

But here's what we need to understand. It's not just you who gets nervous about things at times. EVERYONE does! Your favourite singer or band was probably nervous when they did their first big gig and your favourite sportsperson is likely to be nervous before an important competition or when they're playing in a final.

And guess what? Even teachers can get nervous too! If you don't believe me, ask them. Get them to tell you how they felt on their very first day as a teacher at a new school. Ask other adults you know: 'Has there ever been a time in your life when you felt nervous?' I would be really surprised if they said 'never'.

I can still get a little nervous when I'm speaking at big conferences. But if I want to avoid the nerves, I would have to say no to life's opportunities

rather than

Here's one way to think about it.

Now lots of things we do on a daily basis will feel fine, but sometimes we will need to do something that's out of our comfort zone. We will need to sttttrrreeetttccchhh ourselves.

And that might make us feel nervous and a little anxious, which we know is OK. But those feelings usually won't last too long . . . and remember, you're only feeling the way you do because you want to experience something new and are saying

 to life. 😊

And that's far more exciting than staying in your comfort zone all the time.

Here's the deal.

Life is full of opportunities and experiences, but sadly some people will never enjoy them because they prefer to take the safe, easy option and stay in their comfort zone. As a result, they won't have felt nervous, but neither will they have felt the excitement of doing something new.

And that's a real shame, don't you think?

Here's another reason why we don't always take action.

2. Fear of Failure.

OK, let's be clear, no one, and I mean no one, likes to look stupid and embarrass themselves – unless they are doing it deliberately to get laughs.

But if you try something for the first time, you might not succeed straight away. And that's normal.

When the Scottish tennis player Andy Murray picked up a tennis racket when he was a young child, he didn't serve an ace straight away. Ed Sheeran wasn't an amazing guitarist from the moment he picked up a guitar. And when you were learning to walk, you would stumble and fall down over and over again. But you didn't say:

'I'm hopeless at walking, I'll stick to crawling.'

No, here's what you did.

You persevered. You kept trying. You didn't quit.

And eventually you were able to walk.

But as we get older, and particularly in our teenage years, we become more self-conscious and sensitive to other people's opinions of us – especially our friends.

So it can be really tempting not to push yourself – because if you don't try, you won't fail.

Which is true.

But so is this – if you never try, you will never have the chance to succeed.

little S.U.M.O. Thought

When you avoid the possibility of a setback you also avoid the opportunity for success

A few years ago, my friend Julie told me she was going to write a book. It was at the same time I was writing my SUMO book for adults. You may remember my book was rejected THIRTEEN times by various publishers. That's a lot of fails.

Guess how many rejections Julie has had?

None. Why?

Because she has never contacted a publisher with her book idea.

The outcome? She's never failed – but she's never succeeded either. (She's still a great friend though!)

Here's the final reason we will explore as to what prevents people taking action.

3. Waiting for the right feeling. ...

Alongside writing books, I also work as a 'motivational speaker'. But can I let you into a secret?

There are lots of times in life when I don't feel motivated.

Ssh. Don't tell everyone!

Seriously though, most days I don't wake up screaming 'Yippee it's Monday, bring it on!' For a start I'd scare the cats, Louis and Milo, and I don't think my wife Helen would enjoy being woken by such a greeting either . . . especially as I usually wake up two hours before her!

When I go to the gym on a cold, dark winter's morning, I don't feel especially excited at the thought of scraping the ice off my car window before jumping into a freezing car and driving to the gym.

And as I'm writing this book while still working on a number of other projects (the main one being my long chats with Louis and Milo every morning), I rarely feel creative or full of ideas about what to write.

But here's the thing.

I do go to the gym and I still get up early to write this book.

Why?

**Because I'm not allowing my feelings
to determine my actions.**

But, frustratingly, some people stay stuck and fail to take the action they need to take because they don't feel like it.

And I get that.

Our Red Cap Brain likes to receive immediate satisfaction. It's emotional and likes rewards that happen now, not sometime in the future. And if the Red Cap Brain doesn't feel like doing something, then it's pretty persuasive at convincing us not to. After all, most of us like the easy life, don't we?

But that's not where the magic happens, is it? If it was, we'd all be experiencing the magic. But many of us aren't. And one of the reasons is, we've convinced ourselves – and adults do this just as much as young people – that unless we have the right feelings and really want to do something,
then we won't do it. 🙁

But wouldn't it be great if we learnt that even if we didn't feel like doing something, we managed our Red Cap Brain in such a way that we still did it and learnt to manage our feelings rather than them manage us?

So that's three reasons why we stay stuck, avoid action, and then miss out on the magic.

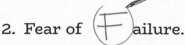

LET'S JUST REMIND OURSELVES OF THOSE THREE REASONS AGAIN.

1. We don't like to feel uncomfortable.

2. Fear of ailure.

3. Waiting for the right feelings.

Which one did you relate to most?

They're actually quite similar, aren't they? They are all to do with our feelings – the **Red** Cap part of our brain. They're like three members of the same family – they're all related.

The question is, now what?

Do we just accept our **Red** Cap Brain is more dominant than our **Blue** Cap Brain and accept the inevitable?

No way!

So read on to discover five ways to make the magic happen.

Are you ready?

Just as sports teams rely on tactics to win games, we are going to look at some tactics to make sure we achieve success in life.

Ever gone on a holiday? I didn't go on many as a teenager, but hopefully most of us get at least a few days away either in this country or abroad. When we do so, unless it's a special surprise, most of us know where we're going before we get there. I doubt many of us set out on our journey without at least one person knowing where we're going.

Can you imagine if that wasn't the case? Imagine turning up at an airport and being asked where you're flying to and answering, 'I don't know, we haven't decided', or getting in a car and the person driving has no idea where they're going.

It would be a bit weird, wouldn't it?

Here's my point.

When you go on holiday, you start with your destination in mind. You know where you want to get to.

That's actually a great metaphor for life: *'Know your destination before you start travelling.'*

Now you often do this already, but without always realising it.

Let me explain.

Here's an example of when you already picture your destination.

Imagine you and your friends have a free weekend. You want to do some fun things together – that's your destination – so you make plans as to what you're going to do and where you're going to go.

You immediately feel good, thinking about what you have to look forward to, don't you?

And there's a reason why you feel that way. Our Red Cap Brain gets excited at the thought of good things happening, which is why I talk to people about the phrase we mentioned earlier:

'Don't hope for happy times, plan them.'

Now on occasions, what we plan to do doesn't happen and sometimes the journey to our destination – like going on holiday – can be affected by delays and cancellations. You may have your own goals for the future, but reaching them might mean having to revise lots or train and practise even when you don't feel like it.

But just remember this.

Your hard work and practice are the route to your success and achievement.

That's why having goals is good as they give you the focus you need to get what you want and reach your destination.

And goals are important in all areas of your life. They can be goals about what you're going to do at the weekend; what item of clothing you're going to buy, but need to save up for; or more long-term goals about what you want to do when you leave school – which I realise might still be some time away.

However, when you do get to that point of sitting exams, think of what doing well in them could mean for you. Picture your destination. Remember the exam is not your destination, but a route to helping you get where you want to go – perhaps an apprenticeship, college, university or a new job.

It's great when you enjoy what you're doing and are engaged in your learning, but if ever you're struggling, or finding you've lots of work that you don't always enjoy, give yourself a little pep talk. Maybe something like 'Doing well in this subject, or completing this project, will mean I get to . . .'

What you achieve will lead to you having more choices in the future. It can lead to you having more opportunities and as a result being able to say **YESSS!** to more things in life.

Your success could also mean you're in a better position to help other people who maybe haven't had the opportunities or support that you've had.

So keep in mind your destination, the goal you want to achieve and picture how you'll feel when you get there.

S.U.M.O. Challenge

Talk to your friends about what exciting things you're looking forward to doing when you're older. Where would you like to travel to? What would you like to become good at? What would you like to try for the first time? Notice how you feel when you talk about these things.

TACTIC 2

Have A
Support Team

I do a lot of driving. I drive tens of thousands of miles every year. But I enjoy a lot of the travelling. Why? Because I have 'someone' to share the journey with. That's sometimes my wife Helen (the cats get car sick, so they tend to stay at home), but sometimes the 'someone' is music, a podcast or the radio.

Here's my point.

When you're on the journey towards your goals in life, it's easier when you don't travel alone. You see, we all need support at times.

little S.U.M.O. Thought

Mates Matter,
Massively

Sometimes, it's your mates who can cheer you up, and knowing they are on the same journey as you and facing similar challenges in life can make things a little easier. Hopefully you can be a support to each other, and working together as a group to learn and discover new things can be really enjoyable – which the Red Cap Brain appreciates.

Your teachers are part of your support team too. OK, you may enjoy being taught by some teachers more than others (I certainly had my favourites when I was at school), but they can all be a great help. They can help you gain the knowledge you need and also challenge you to stretch yourself to achieve your potential.

little S.U.M.O. Thought

Teachers are **M.A.D.** They're. . . **M**aking **A D**ifference

Do you ever wish your teachers didn't give you so much homework?

I could be wrong, but I'm guessing you answered 'Yes' to that question.

OK, so let's imagine whether you're at school or learning an instrument, or playing a sport, that every lesson or practice is super easy.

Lots of laughs, but no learning.

Lots of free time, but no challenge.

Lots of doing easy stuff, but never making progress.

Guess what the consequences of that would be? Short-term pleasure to begin with, but long-term pain ultimately.

Why?

You're not growing. You're not being stretched. You're not achieving your potential.

That's not a great destination, is it?

So, make sure you have people to support you and help you to aim high both in and outside school. And if you need help: ask. Seriously, it's not great struggling alone. You see, we all need to say **YESSS!** to encouraging and supporting one another, and also **YESSS!** to asking for help when we need it.

Seeking support is not a sign of weakness - it's a sign that you're really smart

There's an old joke that says: 'How do you eat an elephant?'

The answer?

One bite at a time.

(Remember, it's a joke – no elephants were harmed in the making of that joke, I promise.)

But there's a message behind the joke. The elephant is huge, you can't eat it all at once, only one mouthful at a time. The same goes for when I'm driving. The trip might be a hundred miles, but I get there one mile at a time.

OK, so what have elephants and my driving got to do with you?

Well at times you might feel overwhelmed by how much you have to do. (My daughter Ruth often felt that way when it came to tidying her bedroom!) When the challenge seems so big, you just don't know where to begin. It can feel overwhelming.

Are you feeling motivated when you feel overwhelmed? Probably not. And remember, some people won't do anything if they don't feel motivated.

But that's not you, is it?

So make it easy for yourself. Don't try and do everything at once.

The task may be big – but it's OK to start small

You're not trying to eat the whole elephant in one go (remember it's a joke, elephants are lovely) and neither are you trying to do all you need to do at once.

The key to making the magic happen?

Just start it.

Don't worry about finishing it. Don't worry about how much you have to do. Your goal to begin with is to just start.

Are you ready to start? Possibly not.

Are you motivated to start? Not always.

But will you start? 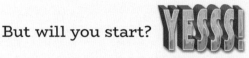 YOU WILL.

And do you know why you will start? Because you've
learnt the following. . .

Right Feelings Follow Right Actions

When I start my car journey, I know there's a long
way to go. But even after just five minutes of driving,
the destination is a little closer. Yes, I know it's
still a long way to go, but I've made a start and I'm
moving. ☺ And after thirty minutes, I'm beginning
to see the progress I'm making.

The same goes for you too. Whatever the task is
that you need to do, start taking bite size actions
and you'll begin to make progress, and your
Red Cap Brain loves it when it feels it's making
progress. You feel good when that happens and
feeling good encourages you to keep on going ☺.

Let me tell you something you already know.

Not every day is a great day. Agree? Not every project you do is a success. Not everything you plan, happens. You're not always the star player in the team or actor in the play. And not every journey you take goes smoothly.

As I've discovered on some of my journeys, sometimes there are delays, cancellations, speed bumps, accidents, diversions, and, on occasions, my sat nav seems more confused than I am as to where we're going! And even when my sat nav is working fine, I sometimes don't follow it's instructions and take the wrong exit at the roundabout, by mistake. Doh!

So what do I do then?

Pull over to the side of the road and abandon my journey? Tell myself I'm a hopeless driver and I'll never get to my destination? Tell myself this always happens to me and no one else and I'm such a loser?

Or . . .

Do I have a kinder conversation with myself and remind myself it was a

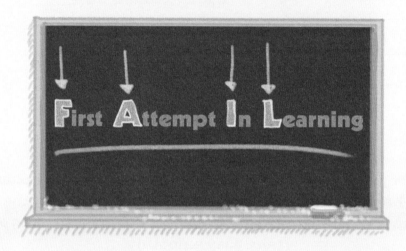

I'm still on the journey. My sat nav will reroute.
I may need to do a 'U-turn' if possible.
But guess what?

I'm still on the way to my destination.

I'm not going to quit. I'm not going to abandon my journey just because it's taking longer to get there than I anticipated.

And that's what you need to remember too. Things don't always go according to plan. It happens to EVERYONE, not just you. But this is not the time to quit – it's the time to press on and persevere.

Have you ever been quick
to quit something you were
doing? Is there something you
have given up doing where you
think it might be good to try
again and keep persevering?
Maybe that's something you
could start doing again, really
soon. What do you think?

TACTIC 5

Enjoy Your Rest
and Reward Stops

It's really important to take action in life, but make
sure you enjoy the journey and get some rest and
reward stops along the way.

When I drive to Scotland from Warrington, a trip that usually takes over three hours, I always take a break on my journey. Sometimes I need to refuel with petrol and, even if I don't, I take a brain break, stretch my legs, and visit the toilet. (Which considering the amount of water I drink when I'm driving is an absolute necessity!)

In life, you need to do the same. Take a brain break, refuel, and hydrate. If you've been sat down a long time, get up and move about – and if you can grab some fresh air too, even better.

Working without a break is like driving a car for too long. Eventually you get tired and become less alert. It's hard to concentrate. My body is telling me I need a break and I'd be really stupid to ignore it.

The same goes for you. Plan breaks when you're studying or working on a project. Give yourself a little treat when you do so. Remember your Red Cap Brain likes to be kept happy, so reward your progress.

I spent ninety minutes writing this chapter and then stopped. I made myself a cappuccino and took some time to check out social media. But I did this AFTER I had done ninety minutes writing, not before. It was a little treat for the progress I'd made and a welcome break for my brain.

What treats or little rewards could you plan to look forward to when you've been studying, training, practising a musical instrument or tidying your bedroom?

What would your treats or little rewards be?

One way to remember the ideas we've discussed in this tactic is to use the following acronym:

Rehydrate and refuel – drink fluid regularly – preferably not a sugary drink, and enjoy a little snack.

Earn the break – treat yourself after you've started, not before.

Stretch your body. Get up and move for a few minutes.

Take time out to do something different from what you've been doing.

SO, IN THIS FINAL SUMO SECRET, WE'VE EXPLORED THREE REASONS WHY WE DON'T ALWAYS TAKE ACTION:

 We don't like to feel uncomfortable.

Fear of (F)ailure.

Waiting for the right feelings.

And then we looked at five tactics to make sure we are taking action and saying to life and all that it offers.

HERE ARE THOSE FIVE TACTICS AGAIN:

1. Picture your destination.

Have a goal and an idea about what you want to achieve.

2. Have a support team.

Your mates matter massively, as do lots of other people in your life, so don't try and do everything on your own. Get the support and encouragement you need to help you towards your goals.

3. Start with bite size actions.

Focus on small steps and aim to make progress, no matter how small, towards your goal. Remember, small steps repeated often can take you a long way. (Oh and be kind to elephants while you're at it ☺.)

4. Don't quit too quick.

Don't allow a setback or disappointment to de-rail you. It happens to everyone. Dust yourself down and get back on track.

5. Enjoy rest and reward stops.

Make sure you enjoy the journey. Give yourself a break, don't burn out. It's OK to chill sometimes and it's good to reward yourself when you've worked hard.

BLUE CAP BRAIN REFLECTION

Review the five tactics to help you take action. Which ones will it be particularly helpful for you to be more aware of?

It's easy at times to read or to hear something, think it's helpful, and then forget about it in a few days. If you're like me, then you need reminders of what you need to remember.

S.U.M.O. Challenge

so...

How about you create a postcard or a poster with the key messages you want to remember from this secret and put it in a place where you'll see it every day. Remember, it's not about how impressive it looks, it's about how helpful it is. (I'm actually looking at a postcard in my office as I write, with three questions on it that I like to ask myself every day.)

One of the points in this SUMO Secret was 'Have a support team'. Mates matter massively and I wonder if there's a mate of yours who might appreciate some support at the moment? (Maybe you could talk to them about some ideas you've learnt from this book or simply send them a message to say hi.)

A Quick *Goodbye* From Me

So our time together is almost over and the first book that I've ever written for young people is almost at an end. I've really enjoyed writing it and I hope you've enjoyed reading it too – and maybe even smiled occasionally.

Above all, I hope you've found the Six SUMO Secrets of real help. Let's briefly remind ourselves of what they were.

We started off with
'There's Something Amazing Inside You'

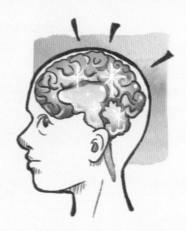

and learned all about our Red Cap (Fast) Brain and our Blue Cap (Slow) Brain. I've only learnt about those ideas in the last few years, but I've found them really helpful. Be aware that lots of adults, including parents and teachers, won't have the knowledge you now have about the brain – unless you let them read your book!

'The Magic Formula'

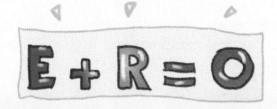

$$E + R = O$$

is something that helps me every day. The Event plus my Response influences the Outcome is a formula I hope every young person learns about, and always remembers.

Our third SUMO Secret was 'The Most Important Person You'll Ever Talk to is . . .'

Make sure you have kind conversations with yourself. If you want a PDF of the seven questions mentioned in that secret, email Yesss@ thesumoguy.com and we'll send you the link.

Our fourth Secret was '**Hippos Do it and So Should You.**' Wallowing for a while is OK – make sure it doesn't last too long though!

Hippo Time is OK!

I hope you found the fifth Secret '**Don't Forget Your Beachball**' helpful. It's not always easy to see someone else's perspective; and communicating with adults when you're a teenager isn't always easy. So I'd love to hear from you about how this SUMO Secret helped you.

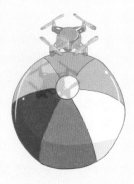

Then there's our sixth and final Secret, '**Making the Magic Happen**'. It's great to have dreams, goals and ideas, but ultimately what counts is not just thinking about things, but actually doing something. If you want satisfaction, you have to take **ACTION**.

Finally, I think it's really important you remember this.

Although you're young, this is your time.

In a few years (hopefully quite a few years), I won't be around anymore – but you will be, and so will the SUMO Secrets.

So please make sure you use them to help yourself, but also others too, so that loads of people on this planet can say **YESSS!** to opportunities, **YESSS!** to making a difference, and an absolutely huge **YESSS!** to life!

Share the secrets!

Thanks, Paul

Paul McGee – The Sumo Guy 2020

CAN I ASK A SMALL FAVOUR PLEASE?

If you enjoyed this book and found it helpful, can you help me spread the SUMO Secrets so more people hear about them?

One way would be to leave a review on Amazon. If you've never left a review before, it's really easy to do, but if you'd prefer someone older than you to do it on your behalf, that's fine too.

Why's it helpful?

Well, people who are thinking of buying the book are keen to know what others thought – it's a bit like Trip Advisor, or a review site for a film. It's hard for them to make a decision though, if there aren't many reviews. So writing one really matters.

You don't have to write an essay either! Just a couple of lines (or more if you prefer) and give it a rating. It would really mean a lot to me if you could. Thanks.

Just go to Amazon.co.uk, type in my name Paul McGee and the title of the book, *Yesss!* Then scroll down till you find 'leave a review' and that's it.

Once you've done so, drop me and the team an email to yesss@thesumoguy.com so we can thank you personally. It really is appreciated.

Thanks again

Paul (plus the cats, Louis and Milo)

YESSS! TO SAYING

THANKS
TO OTHERS

One of my little SUMO thoughts highlights the benefits of asking others for help. In order to write this book, that's exactly what I've done. So I wanted to publicly thank the following people for all their advice and wisdom – this is a better book because of them.

In no particular order, let me start with the Hollamby family: Ed, Sarah, Harriet and Reuben. You've become so closely intwined in the SUMO journey and your passion for all things S.U.M.O. is humbling – thank you. I really valued your feedback as a family on the book.

Catriona Hudson, I love working with you and you're one of the wisest people I know – I've huge respect for your insights, which you share in abundance. Thanks also to Élise Lucía, the oldest teen to read the book – your input was so helpful.

My gratitude to my mate Drew Povey is overflowing – one of the most inspiring and encouraging people I've had the privilege to know. I'm also grateful to your sons Fin and Tom Povey for their perspectives on the book – cheers guys.

I'm really grateful to Kate Middleton and your daughter Lia and also to Tom and Rebecca Palmer – you've each brought your own unique perspective to the book and hopefully its appeal is greater as a result.

Thank you to my friends Andy and Ruth Gee for all your feedback and insights based on a combined total of over 50 years working with young people; and also to Naomi Siddle and Jean Barlow who, despite hardly knowing me, were happy to share their wisdom as teachers.

Richard Gerver, you've been an amazing cheerleader for my SUMO message, as has Kevin Pace. Kevin, your work in developing the SUMO4Schools Foundation (www.SUMO4schools.com) will be brilliant in helping to further develop the SUMO Secrets for young people.

Millie Lloyd, I'm delighted you were a fan of my original SUMO book for adults, even though you were only 10 when you read it! Thank you for your encouragement to me in writing this version.

My appreciation also goes to Kev Daniels and Sally Blackburn-Daniels: I hope you both know how much I value your wisdom.

Helen McGee, your support in every area of my life is constant and I'm grateful for your insights on this book – where would I be without you?

(Lost for sure!)

Finally, I want to say thank you to the illustrator of this book, Fiona Osborne, and also your son Django for his insights as the first teenager to read the manuscript. Fiona, we worked together on my first SUMO book and your illustrations have become iconic. There is no doubt in my mind that you've created some wonderful illustrations for this book which will become equally iconic. It has been so enjoyable working with you again. Thank you.

Paul McGee 2020

MORE BOOKS BY PAUL McGEE:

S.U.M.O. (Shut Up, Move On):
The Straight-Talking Guide to Succeeding in Life, 10th Anniversary Edition

9780857086228

£10.99

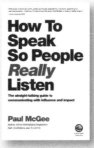

How to Speak So People *Really* Listen:
The Straight-Talking Guide to Communicating with Influence and Impact

9780857087201

£10.99

How to Have a Great Life:
35 Surprisingly Simple Ways to Success, Fulfillment and Happiness

9780857087751

£9.99

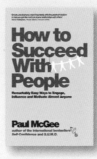

How to Succeed with People:
Remarkably Easy Ways to Engage, Influence and Motivate Almost Anyone

9780857082893

£10.99

Self-Confidence:
The Remarkable Truth of How a Small Change Can Boost Your Resilience and Increase Your Success, 10th Anniversary Edition

9780857088352

£12.99

S.U.M.O. Your Relationships:
How to handle not strangle the people you live and work with

9781841127439

£12.99

How Not To Worry:
The Remarkable Truth of How a Small Change Can Help You Stress Less and Enjoy Life More

9780857082862

£10.99

Stay in touch with Paul:

⌾ @thesumoguy

🐦 @thesumoguy

www.theSUMOguy.com

CAPSTONE
A Wiley Brand

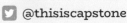

🐦 @thisiscapstone